T0352363

To Kristin, Tilly, and Oscar:
thank you for supporting me and letting me take the time
to make this and bring it into the world. I won't forget it.
I love you.

CONTENTS

INTRODUCTION

The Novel, the Game, and the Long Road to
Legitimacy—The Specificity of Video Games and How
We Should Talk about Them

A couple of years ago, maybe around 2018, a friend of mine was working at a fairly small middle school in Southern California. He really liked his job and was able to connect with the kids since he was willing and capable of handling modern technology. He told me that teachers had no real idea who their students were anymore, which, to be totally fair, is not exactly a new or unique concern for teachers. Since time immemorial, teachers have assumed that their students have the same experiences that they did when they were young and have received for that assumption a sea of totally checked-out faces staring back at them. No kid, in other words, is really *like* their teacher and vice versa.

But this was something more, and it had to do with what kids were watching and consuming, media-wise, when they went home. This too isn't exactly news, as my teachers and I hadn't watched the same TV shows, either. But, he went on, this wasn't an issue of taste or preference: it was an issue of radically divergent content— his students, he told me, weren't going home to binge Netflix. They were going home to spend hours watching Twitch streams, which are channels focused strictly on a single streaming personality or streaming group, like a combination of a Facebook or Twitter profile and a TV channel.

Twitch, for anyone who doesn't know, is primarily for people who play video games regularly (whom we'll refer to as "gamers," albeit an inexact designation) to display their gaming, often to a large audience. There are streams that focus on peoples' everyday lives and of course some fun diversions like Twitch karaoke, but the primary function of Twitch is to connect people who are entertaining or who are very good at gaming to an audience of people who are incredibly interested in watching them do what they do best. Consider it like an online version of the one friend you knew who was really good at making trick shots, in basketball or *Halo*, except with an audience of potentially hundreds of thousands.

And although Twitch allows anyone with the means to stream their gaming freely, the streams that my friend's students were watching were almost certainly the Twitch stars who pull in a serious viewership and income from playing and streaming video games. People watch these streams because these people are often playing at a near-professional level—as, most famously, the player Tyler "Ninja" Blevins does in *Fortnite*—or because they are entertaining regardless of gameplay—as with the half-comedy, half-gaming streaming collective, the Go off Kings. But the main difference between these streamers and the TV and film stars of the past is that their viewers aren't watching them to vicariously live a life they could not. Instead, they're watching them play a game (at least when it comes to popular stream games like *Fortnite*) that many of them could and *do* play themselves.

This seemed weird to me at the time, as it may seem strange to you if you're of a certain age when most gaming was done in a physically connected and limited space. The worst thing to me as a kid was watching a friend play a game who didn't give me a turn to play; the most tempting thing was to never give my friends a turn playing. Asking for one more turn to try to beat a level in *Super Mario Brothers* when I was six and my friend was desperate to try the weird new underground level; watching my cousins play *Castlevania II* and wanting a taste of that strange, gothic world and not getting one; playing at a new friend's house just to see what the Playstation thing was all about and getting only that small taste of the *Crash Bandicoot* demo; not wanting to give up the controller until you got over that one hump in *Street Fighter 3rd Strike* or *Tekken* or *Mario Kart*—these were the kinds of feelings I experienced. Gaming with friends was, at its core, a power struggle for the controller, and watching wasn't just less fun, it was, for most, not fun at all—it was an utter deferral and denial of satisfaction. So you can understand my confusion.

The difference here is that Twitch is not about the gaming itself: it's not a space that primarily values the actual inputting of mechanics into a video game interface. Put another way, you wouldn't ask baseball spectators why they don't just go outside and play baseball themselves; the two activities have completely different appeals, even for professional or semiprofessional players. Playing the game is an active use of energy and engages a kind of adrenal push for participation; watching, on the other hand, is a passive engagement with the culture of sport, a more social and relaxing activity. What I and a bunch of other thirtysomethings out there had missed, in other words, was that gaming now had what sports does: a reason to engage socially, outside of the game itself.

The way games developed this culture is a longer story than this book can deliver—and probably one that can't be told in a single book. In part this is because the popularity and cultural emergence of gaming has a lot to do with the development of gaming technology, the internet, and the rapidly distanced culture we all engage in now. But the mostly untold story involves how the act of gaming shifted away from the individual action of play and refocused on the communal experience we see in the popularity of Twitch gaming. Specifically, this story is about how gaming as a medium of cultural expression was shaped specifically by the reaction of its fans, more so than perhaps any other medium in the twentieth and twenty-first centuries.

Or, to frame this like a question: Is the fact that we are as happy to watch games being played as we are to play them ourselves due to how gaming has changed or due to how we are changing gaming? Does the audience determine the product when it comes to video games, or are we being driven along by the industry? As we see, both the developer and the audience share the responsibility of creating the current cultural moment in gaming, and this revelation can show us that we, as an audience, have the ability to impact how that moment changes moving forward. But before we go forward, let's go back just a bit, to circa 325 BCE.

* * *

Video games are now and have always been on the cultural defensive. From their introduction in the home through the Atari 2600, they have been viewed as a waste of time or a frivolity. Further back, they served as the fun counterpart to the real computational revolution—Deep Blue, the famous early supercomputer that took on chess grandmaster Garry Kasparov, may have been playing a game, but the match counted for industrial, political, and, most importantly, economic stakes; your average game of *Pong* did not. The intelligence that could be marshaled by supercomputers promised advances in automation, calculation, and efficiency, after all. In comparison, the gaming that invaded the home and arcade marketplace might have had profit-making potential for its creators, but it was ultimately considered a pastime in the tradition of whist or charades—unremarkable at best, actively distracting and trivializing at worst.

But there's more to the story than productivity and profit when it comes to cultural and social impact. Indeed, the consistent presence of cultural objects that are in and of themselves unproductive has been a fact of life throughout recorded history. Human beings need recreation to balance the daily work they have to do to survive and prosper materially, and the truly impractical life of the mind is the place where this recreation takes place when people are unsuited to or uninterested in physical play. And so the poetry, novels, and games that occupy the mind and shock the productive conscience proliferate even as they are attacked by their cultural and moral critics. These attacks have roots that are millennia old.

In his *Republic*, written around 325 BC, the Greek philosopher Plato recounts a dialogue involving his teacher Socrates in which Socrates explains why poetry needs to be heavily censored in any perfect state. Plato and Socrates are, as is typical, on the same page about this, and much of current cultural critique takes its inspiration from these two ancient philosophers, particularly concerning "imitation." For both philosophers, imitation is a philosophical problem because it cannot fully replicate the model it means to reproduce. Even if I take an ideal chair as a model for my attempt to build a chair as an untrained carpenter, for instance, the latter will not live up to the former—neither in function nor appearance. Similarly, Plato and his teacher tell us, the poet or author's imitations of reality cannot live up to the model of truth. Since a young mind "takes the impression that one wishes to stamp upon it," any sort of lie that could influence those young minds away from truth should not be told.[1]

In the typical nature of a Socratic dialogue, the question-and-answer cadence regarding truth and representation leads us down the road very quickly to "a censorship over our storytellers."[2] And if this all sounds a bit antiquated to you, maybe Socrates's reasoning will sound a bit more contemporary. He argues that stories should be sanitized and free of satire or ambiguity because "the young are not able to distinguish what is and what is not allegory."³ This line of thinking—that children won't or can't distinguish between fantasy and reality—is what drives almost all reactive critique against media, from Fredric Wertham's screed against comic books in *The Seduction of the Innocent* to Jack Thompson's decades-long campaign against video games. Most recently, Thompson could have been paraphrasing Plato and Socrates when in 2018 he said of a recent mass shooting, "What happens in the case of heavy users of video games is that when they have the virtual reality taken from them, they will set out to make it real reality."⁴

So we see our cultural critics from 325 BC and AD 2018 both insisting that the reality we live in can and will be tainted by the imitated realities we consume and also that only morally and factually true media can instruct us and aid our journeys as productive citizens. Video games and television, even more than novels, poems, films, or plays, fall directly into this critique: dangerous fluff that by virtue of their ubiquitous, everyday presence in our lives hides the nature of the world from us more effectively than any previous entertainment technology.

This distrust has not, of course, curbed their popularity, and video games enjoy increasing relevance in our current moment as Twitch streaming, e-sports celebrities like Ninja and FaZe Clan, and the rise of digital downloads make video games more popular and more accessible than ever. But the moral panic that accompanies the Platonic concerns does not mean that right-wing or traditionalist politics are straying away from video games; to the contrary, video games as a genre are becoming more and more reactionary as time goes on, representing or misrepresenting reality in service of paranoia and power as opposed to progressivism or distancing. This is important, too, because although we've given a lot of time to how imitation is viewed by its critics, imitation is also the only way to imagine better or different realities. That these realities could be imagined in both a progressive *and* a reactionary sense is something that hasn't been given enough attention by people who want to understand the cultural potential of games: the future of video games isn't necessarily the homogeneity of reactionary patriotism and fear. There are paths that we have yet to imagine the medium taking.

This book aims to try to imagine those paths yet traveled and provide a progressive audience a reason to care about a medium that is so often given over to angry young white men in popular media. Though we've come a long way from puritanical valuations of "hard work" as a virtue in and of itself, self-care culture is still laser focused on efficiency and production, and the embarrassment over the frivolity of leisure hasn't entirely disappeared. As a result, gaming is typically seen as frivolous and inessential, and although it certainly is unproductive in a real sense, there is no reason to abandon gaming as a toxic dead end without exploring both its history and its potential as a cultural medium uniquely receptive to its audience. If we are to imagine alternative political worlds from a progressive and, yes, leftist perspective, the simultaneity of reception, critique, and revision that is taking place in gaming today provides the best place to think beyond the seemingly impossibly firm limits of our political and cultural present. Because imitation doesn't always erode the model from which it draws, it also can surpass it as well.

I'm going to try to prove this point by considering the ways that famous gaming series have changed over time as they initially make their claims, are taken in by a mass of fans who interpret those claims in their own ways, and are finally reimagined, the later entries in the series doing their own form of imitative reproduction of the earlier. This feedback process of production-reception-reproduction is one that I think is unique to serialized media, and the length of time that some of these properties cover makes video games in particular of great interest to this analysis. The *Final*

Fantasy series, one of our objects here, is thirty-three years old and counting; the genre of the battle royale shooter, our youngest and most diverse group of games by far, is at its youngest, seven years old already. A lot of time has passed between the earliest games in this book and the most recent, and that has allowed these series to change, often in dramatic ways, from their original projects. How we view their politics and aesthetics—which are, to my mind, political in and of themselves—is changing, and how we might work to influence them in the future is what this book strives to answer.

But before we get to gaming, I want to take a trip back in time and briefly consider another upstart media genre that upset a great many people, seemed like it would change the world with its progressive politics, and took a mass audience by storm before proving to be as conservative if not more so than any other genre that had preceded it. That's right, let's talk about the novel.

* * *

When scholars refer to the "birth of the novel," it's important to remember that there is no single "first novel" to which they're referring. The murky soup of the novel's origins is mixed up with poetry, short fiction, travelogues, and the strange ambitions of eighteenth-century writers. This isn't a book of literary criticism, so I won't bore you with my readings of Ian Watt or Michael McKeon (though the authors themselves certainly are worth your time), but the novel itself has a lot to teach us about the nature of video games and their potential as a medium. Both have been roundly dismissed as trivial, brain-rotting uses of time in their own moment. Both are typically enjoyed by younger, more impressionable people, which makes authority figures then and now nervous. And both have grown to some sort of maturity amid a hugely controversial tug-of-war between the people who would define them as media.

You could argue that in the eighteenth century, Daniel Defoe's *Robinson Crusoe* was the beginning of the novel and that novels were at their core fictional stories of adventure, danger, and a strange economic wit. Someone might respond that you are a fool, that novels should look like Samuel Richardson's *Clarissa*, a series of fictional letters between characters both in love and in danger of losing their virtue to love. And a third person could argue that novels were morality tales mixed with the kind of epic structure we see in Homer, à la *Tom Jones* by Henry Fielding. A fourth person might stop you in your tracks and say that the novel is meant as a satirical experiment, like the wondrous and confounding *Tristram Shandy* by Laurence Sterne. And all of these arguments would be right in some respects and wrong in others—the novel contains multitudes and is at various times adventurous, scandalous, edifying, experimental, and, more often than not, entertaining.

Consider the same kind of debate around video games in the late 1970s and early 1980s. Roberta Williams might tell you that her new game *Mystery House* was the future of the video game genre, with branching narrative paths, a progression of ever-more extravagant ways to die, and rudimentary but remarkably evocative graphics. Will Crowther might interrupt her and say that his game, *Colossal Cave Adventure*, with its confounding mazes, engaging adventure, and mental difficulty combined with textual flair was the way things were going. Someone might interject and say that video games were simply a stopping point before electronic art and literature proper merged, which would offer new potential for all three forms. Then Toru Iwatani might peek around the corner and tell you that his new game, *Pac-Man*, was going to revolutionize the world of games, which were, of course, not about stories at all but rather about amassing millions of points in reflex-breaking work. And once again, all of them would be right in a way. But as we look at it from the twenty-twenty vistas of hindsight, we can say none was *exactly* right.

This is because video games, like novels or any type of artistic medium, are somewhat more capacious than their descriptions imply. A novel might be instructive—like, say, the sentimental literature of early America that provided girls with rules for chaste living and horror stories to deter rebellion—but ultimately it has an aesthetic set of concerns behind the instruction, which leaks out of that small descriptive box. A video game might be narrative at its core but still have the kinds of mechanics that encourage speed-runners and competitive-minded gamers to try and overcome the limits of the narrative frame. Similarly, people can bring their own stories to the blank slates of *Robinson Crusoe* and *Pac-Man*, projecting and creating their own realities, which are ultimately no less real or significant than the realities on the page.

In short, these two mediums are related to each other because they resist being defined in any single predictable way despite their popularity and their reach. Even today, four hundred years later, the novel is tricky to pin down as a medium, and video games are getting even more complex than ever. And the dialectic corollary to this inability to pin down the medium for these types of art is that the force behind their meaning expands beyond the stories they tell about themselves and beyond the stories we tell about them. A game's story may be trivial, even silly on its face, but it is almost certainly transformatively important to someone, not in spite of but *because* of that triviality. The tiny plumber who fights turtles or the noble hero trying to save her tiny alien friend, the Metroid, are more than willing to adapt themselves to the story you want them to tell as a player. Well—up to a point.

But instead of telling you about this, as I do in the rest of this book, allow me to share an example of my reading of *Fortnite*.

* * *

Fortnite can somewhat modestly be called a historical worldwide phenomenon. Massively popular, incredibly widespread in its player base, and available to be played on almost any platform for free, the game has earned its parent company Epic Games an ungodly amount of money and allowed it to go toe-to-toe with Apple Store, a feat heretofore unheard of. But beyond its popularity as an intellectual property, the game is about something, too, and involves you playing a character fighting for resources in a gradually shrinking world while trying to kill off the other players before they kill you.

Well, okay, that's what I think it's about anyway.

A couple of years before writing this book, I wrote an article at the (now sadly defunct) Outline titled "*Fortnite* Could Only Exist in a World That's Running out of Resources." I want to revisit the article's argument, at least in part, because I think I was right (naturally) but also because perhaps I was proven wrong in the end by *Fortnite*'s own player base.[5]

So let's start with a bit of a description for those readers who don't have kids or refuse to learn what their kids like: in *Fortnite*, you are dropped from a goofy flying bus onto a cartoonish island with ninety-nine other players. Your goal on the island is twofold: to survive and to build. The survival part is also twofold, as the other players can shoot or axe or explode you to death and a storm encroaches on you from all sides. The storm takes what is a massive map and quickly shrinks it down so that you're forced to face the other deadly players who are trying to be the last one standing.

Meanwhile, the building part is a crucial element of the game. A holdover from when *Fortnite* was conceived and planned as a cooperative game revolving around fortress building against zombie hordes, the building mechanic has been the crowning achievement of the battle royale mode. Cutting down trees, buildings, cars, rocks, and really anything in your way with a pickaxe, your avatar can amass materials and build walls, ceilings, stairs, and more.

Using these constructions, you can bide your time safely as the storm closes in or create an unbreachable vantage point from which to gun down your enemies.

What this unconventional blend of gaming elements—the coordinated violence of *Player Unknown's Battleground* combined with the cartoonish world building of *Minecraft*—produces is an army of Twitch streamers performing acrobatic, operatic maneuvers around each other, building while shooting and dodging upward as a storm surges around them. It has all the hallmarks of a blockbuster, and it's really no wonder that it's been an enormous hit.

But for a game that's deeply popular with the preteen set—thanks in no small part to being free to play as well as for its seamless mobile port—it's a bit strange to see the dramatization of kill-or-be-killed fantasies in bright colors and wacky costumes. *Fortnite* is a totally bloodless and innocent game despite its ostensible murder-for-survival subject matter—a game almost every child plays wherein the basic goal is to murder an entire island full of people and do funny dances.

Let me stop for a moment and say in no uncertain terms that I don't think video games cause violence, nor do I think *Fortnite* is poisoning our kids. As someone asked before I wrote this piece, why spend time taking *Fortnite* to task for dramatizing murder for resources when there are games like *Player Unknown's Battlegrounds* or *Call of Duty: Modern Warfare 4* that have all the elements of *Fortnite* but none of the cartoonish levity? But what's interesting about *Fortnite* isn't the violence of the game itself, but rather the somewhat laissez-faire reaction to the violence by a media apparatus that has largely loosened up, compared with 1999, yet still finds a way to clutch its pearls during every news cycle. *Fortnite*'s violence, in other words, is only interesting because people are not reacting with shock. Instead, they understand that it makes all the sense in the world.

The logic of scarcity asserts that there's a finite number of things in the world that we all need to survive and thrive and only the strong can have them. This is something that we've basically internalized and banished to the background of our mind, only noticing when it is expressed in surprising or blunt ways. One example was a tweet in which Israeli Prime Minister Benjamin Netanyahu justified the use of force against Palestinians who were fomenting against Israeli occupation of their land by tying the idea of the scarcity of land and shelter to violence in "defense" of those resources for Israelis and against Palestinans and was justifiably censured widely. But we casually reiterate the same sentiments daily when we—even those of us on the far left—talk about the ways massive climate change operates not as a structural imperial injustice but as a scientific tragedy. The logic of scarcity is not simply at the root of Netanyahu's brutal proclamation, but also at the core of all of our assumptions about the future of human civilization, about birth rates, about walls around our borders, and about the need to buy land in the Pacific Northwest to avoid being boiled alive: *there's not enough for all of us, so I need to get mine.* Even in our video games.

Once again, though, let's take a step back and acknowledge that when your thirteen-year-old nephew plays *Fortnite* all through Christmas Eve while muttering "thank you" for the Amazon gift certificates he receives, he isn't actively becoming a reactionary fascist or anything. No kid or streamer is thinking of *Fortnite* as some kind of political statement; they're playing it because it's fun and well made. I would even go so far as to wager that Epic Games didn't make *Fortnite* because it thought it could profit from a pernicious logic that undergirds late capitalism. It made its battle royale hit because its fortress-building game flopped and it wanted to save the intellectual property. None of the actors here is performing some sort of deep skullduggery.

But that we have a legitimate cultural phenomenon based on a ritualized kill-or-be-killed game style and no one seems overly concerned about the implications is something that I think is worth noting. Maybe in 1999, the media would have been absolutely frothing about the battle royale's renaissance, but the persistent terror and spectacle of 2021 cast a much larger shadow. This lack of attention, however, may ultimately be why *Fortnite* matters. One benefit of art, historically, has been that it defamiliarizes the world in ways that allow us to recognize our own ingrained behaviors as ridiculous or harmful. When Bertolt Brecht claimed that art wasn't a mirror of reality but a hammer that shapes it, he meant that art and theater have the ability not just to reflect reality, but to distort it as well. *Fortnite* isn't about scarcity, but it could not reach such a level of popularity in a world that wasn't shaped by scarcity. What we recognize in *Fortnite*, at an almost unconscious level, is the logic of our own world reflected back to us. There's comfort in being able to manipulate and control that logic so that we end up on top for once.

So is the end of the story, I asked when I wrote this article, that *Fortnite* is conditioning us to accept the order of the world as a meat grinder that spits out all but the elite? Is this seemingly innocent murder-dance simulator teaching kids that shooting up a school is ephemeral but hoarding the means of survival is forever?

And the answer then and now is, of course not. But what's hard to parse is that this logic is at the core of the game's appeal, and as such *Fortnite* can reveal the paranoia and fear of hoarding and land grabbing in a clear-eyed and disturbing way. As Netanyahu demonstrated, when the tenets behind the logic of scarcity are expressed in starkly Manichaean terms, they aren't as easily normalized as the idea that, for example, there isn't enough food for everyone. If it can make people question why a fight to be the last one standing feels so comfortable in contemporary America or why the natural extension of a battle royale, even for kids, is to acquire bigger guns, then maybe *Fortnite* can be a hammer to shape reality too.

But the distinction that is missed here is that *Fortnite* doesn't shape reality; rather, reality shapes *Fortnite*, or at least its player base does. The game itself may function around the mechanics of violent scarcity and may literally involve the hoarding of wood, stone, and metal to build fortresses that are defended with shotguns, sniper rifles, and more, but the actual *logic* of the game is determined by the psyche of the player base, whose average age is far younger than anyone who cares one iota about global scarcity. Instead, what we see in *Fortnite* is a privileging of the cartoonish, collectable, and event-driven nature of the metagame surrounding the battle royale. Yes, most of the popular *Fortnite* streaming involves the building and the shooting elements of the game, which makes sense from the standpoint of spectatorship. But the actual spectacle of the game is its massive communal quality, with concerts and speeches taking place in-game for players to see as they shoot, build, and dance outside of the confines of the battle royale. Or it's in the recurring gimmicks, rendered as seasons, in which John Wick or Galactus, the devourer of worlds, descends into the world of *Fortnite* to cause some sort of limited-time event.

And, yes, these events and spectacles get the player base to buy the *Fortnite* currency, which is the way this free game makes its ungodly profit. But such events and spectacles also are determined by its player base and their appetites; *Fortnite* operates in that too-rare capitalist synergy that free-market advocates champion: it produces a supply that is bolstered and informed by a demand.

So although the logic of scarcity informs the mechanical rules of the game itself, *Fortnite* has changed over time to become more capacious than its space of play. The game is a social event, a signifier of social capital, and it operates like a meeting spot or a shared reference as much as or more than it operates as a shooter. In this way, the "text" of *Fortnite*—what it is literally *about*—

actually does not tell us much about why the game is popular or what the game accomplishes for its fans and players. Instead, those fans and players *determine* that appeal, changing the game from the inside as readers change a novel by internalizing and personalizing the content.

* * *

Fortnite is, of course, a radical outlier. The game is a free-to-play shooter that turned into a social phenomenon thanks to sudden stream popularity, a killer mobile app, and an audience that absolutely clicked with what Epic Games was producing at exactly the moment it needed that audience to click. Furthermore, the model of profit for Epic Games relies on fan engagement. There's no money in *Fortnite* if players aren't buying the extras, so fan engagement is absolutely *the* most important element to the soup that is the free-to-play battle royale. And finally, *Fortnite* is online, which makes it a social experience ready to be shared on demand by millions at almost any moment during the day, which makes the already volatile "reading experience" of the game's "plot" radically more changeable.

But what is not unique or exceptional about *Fortnite* is the interaction between game and fan itself. As we see in this book, the history of games, particularly of games that are parts of long series or part of a specific genre, is one of creative tension between players and creators. It's of course tempting to read this relationship in a cynical, mercenary way, and certainly we are dealing with massive companies, so that element absolutely exists. However, we're also dealing with the issue of authorial intention and what happens to that intention when it meets readers or, in this case, players.

Because although you may find that hypothetical person willing to argue with you about *Tristram Shandy*, you're far more likely to find someone willing to argue that the novel's figuration of coitus interruptus—both textually and visually through black pages entirely obscured through printer's ink and squiggly illustrations—are postmodern precursors and apt metaphors for the writing process and creation. Is it possible Sterne thought this was the point of his novel when he wrote it? Of course. But is it likely the purpose of *Tristram Shandy* or, moreover, what the novel is *about*?

The answer is yes and also no. Both *Tristram Shandy* and *Fortnite*—a comparison that has M. H. Abrams spinning in his grave as we speak—present the productive quandary of authorial intention meeting an inventive and perhaps unintended audience. I imagine *Fortnite* didn't expect a largely streaming/media crossover audience younger than eighteen, and neither did Sterne intend *Tristram Shandy* to be the novel du jour for academics concerned with the representational quality of textuality. Yet this interplay is part of the patina of both pieces now, a rich layering of intention and reception, all adding to the totality of what these texts are about.

But we can't do much more than say this and move on, observing the interplay and quibbling over which side matters more. That is, we can't do it until we consider the series in gaming. A series refers to a group of games that follows a cycle of sequels, prequels, and additions to a major franchise or, in some specific instances, a group of games that continues to iterate on a particular genre. In these games, we see the same kind of interplay between an intended product and its audience, but we also see an evolution of this interplay over time, as the games respond to their audience, and the audience's opinions respond in kind. In these instances, what we see is not a single interaction, but an evolution—the birth of a trend and an observable change. It is through this change that we can see the potential of what games can do as a medium, as well as the ways in which the medium can fall apart.

What we see on this journey through games is the way that video games can change their audience and also the ways an audience can change a game. Although we may come no closer to determining the medium specificity of games, we will see the ways in which they can serve as avenues of influence, both in terms of their own ability to change as a medium and in terms of their ability to suggest new ways of thinking about our political and cultural landscape.

*** * * ***

In the rest of this book, we'll take a wide-ranging journey through genre and series, stopping to discuss high and low points, optimistic shifts in gaming consciousness, and pessimistic moments of failure. I discuss the creators and the games themselves, putting them in context with what came before, during, and after their development, and, of course, what people had to say about and demand from these games. It is a uniquely revealing journey through the gaming landscape of the past thirty years.

1

SURVIVAL HORROR

What Are You Scared of and What Does It Mean?

What do we most fear? And why? Horror video games are understood as flashpoints of terror for most, and the question of why they are so scary or what they are making a metaphorical terror out of typically falls out of the frame. There are larger ideas that horror draws from and social concerns that animate the trends we see in the media and shake us to our core. Horror games may emblematize this balance between drawing on the world for influence and reproducing these worldly fears as a cathartic release. As we see in this chapter, how these fears evolve can tell us how video games reveal important truths about our society and culture, as well as the ways games themselves help us unpack these fears in ourselves through an aesthetic expression.

* * *

Perhaps the most common observation about the 1980s slasher flick boom is that the whole craze and perhaps the entire subgenre of "crazed madman kills fleeing teens" is a thinly veiled metaphor for sexual conservatism. It's not a bad observation, really, and it can be easily complicated by the realization that we as an audience typically relate less to, say, *Texas Chainsaw Massacre*'s Leather-face than the girl who escapes him. Media critic Carol Clover is generally considered the first major critic to make this turn in her seminal text on horror films, *Men, Women, and Chainsaws*, and she further argues that horror movies actually can allow us a space to explore radical feminist impulses in media. In other words, that *Friday the 13th* marathon you're about to watch isn't all about killing coeds after they just got done having some premarital sex; it's about rooting for the one woman who *escapes* the blood orgy.

Now, there are some critiques of Clover's perspective that are clear even from a cursory reading: How superficial were these emancipatory feminist moments, given that the craze happened at the height of Ronald Reagan's culturally conservative omnipres-ence? Why is it empowering to let one girl live and kill five or six others? And why, in the revenge fantasy spur of the slasher genre, does a woman need to be raped or assaulted in order to claim some kind of agency? Is the claim that the slasher genre is feminist really any easier to dispute than the claim that it's all about sexual repres-sion?

Clover does answer more than a few of these questions, and I'm doing a disservice to her work by being so glib, but it is useful to see how the discourse around horror shifts and distorts around whoever is watching or experiencing the horror themselves. Horror is, at its core, a genre that asks a lot of its audience: it asks that the audience withstand deliberately uncomfortable moments of ten-sion; it asks that its audience bring to bear on the media their own fears so that the scares resonate more deeply; and it asks that view-ers sympathize both with the killer (in order to make the film more interesting) and the victim (in order to make the film more sus-penseful). In short, horror needs its audience to participate actively to succeed as much as, if not more than, any other contemporary genre.

This helps to explain why the modern horror genre is populated with creators who were fans before they were writers, directors, or—in our case—video game developers. The active participation in the framing of horror, as a sort of symbiotic process between the film (or game, novel, etc.) and the audience, empowers a sort of personalized version of terror. More than, say, serious dramatic fare, it's absolutely reasonable if not *necessary* to respond to a horror movie by talking about what it made you feel, how it impacted you, what it made you think it was about. I could argue the "correct" reading of *To Sleep with Anger*, but as critic Sean McTiernan demonstrated recently in his perceptive podcast on found footage horror, *Hundreds of Dead Pixelated Bodies*, one's reaction to something like *The Blair Witch Project* is so colored by personal experience as to make a singularly correct or agreed-upon reading impossible.

All we can really say definitively about the horror genre boils down to three basic truths: horror is expected to scare its audience, whether through jump scares, psychological terror, excessive violence, and so forth; the success of the horror genre depends on keying in to its audience's fears as specifically as possible; and, because of points one and two, horror must reflect back to its audience societal fears that are resonant enough to supersede our individual, discrete experiences of those fears. In other words, the horror genre reflects what its viewers can relate to but does so in such a way that many viewers can have different experiences of that reflection. It's a tough balance, but somehow the horror genre has gotten more and more popular over time, so balance must be possible.

Fortunately for us, we consider only one arm of the massive horror industry: horror video games. Perhaps less fortunately for us, this is still a massive chunk of media, with more and more games coming out daily due to a thriving major market—sometimes referred to as AAA—demand and an industrious independent and amateur development scene making far more games than we could ever cover in one book, let alone one chapter. With this in mind, let's shift our focus to the beginnings of the video game horror genre as we know it, specifically to the birth of the "survival horror" subgenre with the *Alone in the Dark* and *Resident Evil* series. This type of horror game, in which players guide one or more characters out of a terrifying situation with limited health, ammunition, and (often) time, was an innovation that sparked new-found interest in horror games and spoke to a somewhat primal fear of disconnection and loneliness in the late 1990s and early 2000s.

What followed the survival horror genre is harder to pin down, but the horror games of today have shifted from games about being, well, alone in the dark and focus more on fears of being sur-rounded, detected, or "found out." This perhaps comes as no sur-prise in a global environment defined by surveillance: the author-ities aren't the only ones who can determine exactly what you're doing online and in your personal life through closed-circuit televi-sion, social media monitoring, and algorithms that calculate the best way to advertise to your most personal desires. With such a wide-ranging and encompassing set of fears, it is also harder to narrow the focus to specific franchises, so for the sake of this chapter, I abandon that approach here and examine the genre as a whole. With horror games, this may well be the only way to ap-proach them; as fans become creators and as the games shift both to reflect a shared generic past as well as a particular horrific present, horror games shift and change in relation to the other games within in their genre. The genre is reactive this way, and this of course is evident in the ways that certain horror trends dominate the scene for a few months or years before disappearing into history: there are horror themes that are right for a particular moment in time.

In short, horror games reflect the fears of their player base, and those fears evolve with and in reaction to those games. It is a pure expression of the sort of creator-audience feedback loop we see more and more in this medium, and as such, it bleeds beyond the typical series organization. What we will see is that this feedback loop serves not only to anticipate the fears of an upcoming generation of creators, but also to reveal the underlying fears of an often-unheard player base as the tools to make these games become freely available. The horror genre in games haunts its player base, first as a symbiotic leech for feelings of terror and horror and later as a reflective output for negative emotions and fears.

At the center of these fears is capitalist excess: loneliness during moments of plenty and submersion in moments of struggle. How these games reflect and ultimately subvert these fears reveal the political and existential stakes of this genre of game during the last twenty years.

* * *

Horror has been at the core of games since before their digitization, of course, as the vast Ouija board empire indicates. Indeed, the idea of the supernatural conjures the same basic narrative beats as the presence of a mystery or an adventure with an uncertain outcome: as a creative writing professor might intone, it gives the work a sense of risk; it gives it stakes. It's not surprising then that two of the most seminal early horror video games—Roberta Williams's *Mystery House* and Will Crowther's *Colossal Cave Adventure*—are situated in the mystery and suspense genres. Solving a murder and navigating a cave are two very different tasks that, as popular film and media suggest, often boil down to the same thing: trying to stay alive. This gave added exigency to the text-based format of early games, and games like the seminal *Zork* still conjure terror and frustration with small, strange phrases like "you may be eaten by a grue."

The difference, as much as a clearly delineated one exists, between this sort of generic horror and the survival horror that marks the beginning of our focus is that the horror in these early games was subjugated to the task of making these new digital objects. Williams, Crowther, and their many colleagues in the late 1970s and early 1980s created games that absolutely reflected their social moment but were doing so primarily through the lens of technological auteurism or, to put it a different way, as computer prodigies trying to make code do something new and different.

What this "something different" entailed was primarily text garnished with visuals drawn from ASCII and rudimentary graphical software. *Mystery House* had a consistent visual element to it, as your character wandered through the eponymous house, guided by text input, but the visuals of the game were not what you'd expect if you came into it as a gamer from 2021. Rather, the lines and shapes are rendered as choppy approximations, pixelated and abstracted, requiring the player to put a lot of themselves into the work of atmosphere creation.

Colossal Cave Adventure, on the other hand, was at first a fully text-based affair, with the imagined world left entirely to the player, like other early gaming classics like *Zork*. That said, the game inspired future graphical adaptations, including a particularly colorful 1986 release, which more importantly pushed the visualization of mapped space for gamers. Charting your course on graph paper and maintaining a good sense of where you'd been and where you were going was in essence a good way of staying alive in the game's cave environment, but also a way of building an encompassing atmosphere. Just as Williams's *Mystery House* had done, *Colossal Cave Adventure* encouraged players to build a world in a way that had not been done before. As a result, the horror in these games added a sort of narrative spice and was often quite well done in these and more obscure text-based adventures, the point of which was to shift the technological ability of the genre forward so that it could become the kind of expressive and spatially evocative medium we recognize now. Art, then, but more exploratory and curious than much of the work explored here.

The real test of expression in these games and where our analysis can truly begin to take shape, then, would probably be well after *Mystery House* and its architectural experimentation and into the advent of 3D experimentation on the PC, where developers were using polygons to create the illusion of a fully fleshed-out world with not only right, left, up, and down, but forward and backward along a z-axis. In 1992's *Alone in the Dark*, developer Frédérick Raynal of Infogrames produced a horror game that provided a visual element to the sprawling mansions and caves that marked the text-based genre previously. As a result, the game itself has nonlinear maps, traps, and monsters that can surprise and vex the player, and it is the exploration of these tricks and quirks of the 3D world that allow the terror and lasting fear of the game to settle in.

It is tough to get honest reads on many of the older games I cover here, since a cottage industry of rereviewing classics—first in blogs and then on more established websites as a sort of retrospective—means that most reviews begin with an apology or explanation that the game is an established, canonical classic. There's a place for looking back, but when you begin a review with an acknowledgment of the game's history, it's hard to understand how it felt to experience that game when it was released, how it must have felt to play it without any sense of expectation. Although I'm sure newsgroups and message boards buzzed about *Alone in the Dark* in 1992 and 1993, its introduction was long enough from our era that we have to rely on more prosaic archives.

Instead of trusting my own recollection of the game (I was seven, so we probably can't do that reasonably) or trusting others' "accurate" recollections of their reactions years after the fact, let's look at Charles Ardai's whimsical and, most importantly, contemporary-with-the-game in-character review of *Alone in the Dark*, in which he plays a proper old-time corporal who has left a mysterious diary that . . . reviews *Alone in the Dark*.[1] It's difficult to explain what a time capsule this piece is; the earnest, geeky, and ambitious qualities of Ardai's article attempt to tell readers whether the game is worth buying and produces a snapshot of a very different time in video game retail. Magazines like *Computer Gaming World*, where Ardai published his review, used its access to games to sell issues, and readers used that access to determine if a game was worth paying $49.99 for during an era in which a game simply might be too bugged to play on your PC without hours of work. Readers wanted engaging reviews that had a clear bottom line: *Do I want to buy this?* Without the market environment of digital direct sales, emblematized by Valve's "Steam" marketplace and the ascendant Epic Store, in which games continually go on sale due to a lack of material limitations, the consumption of games had to be more circumspect. The snippets people used to decide what to consume were carefully curated and presented by these magazines. So quirky, heavily informational, review-based content was, if not common, not entirely unexpected.

And so it is in this context that Ardai's strange Colonel Lemuel Cork, who both reviews *Alone in the Dark* and leaves clues to his own disappearance within its pages, says the following about the game itself (emphasis mine):

> None of the other simulations I had experienced previously, in my dreams, had this effect. None of the others could stir the heart in my breast, bring me to shortness of breath, make me lean forward in my seat until my face was barely a foot from the glass. None before had made me care about the characters whose lives I directed. None had made me jump in fright at the slightest sound. Nor had any so fully realized an environment: though it only existed on the glass, *I feel that I have been inside a real house*.[2]

It's easy, in retrospect, to argue that Ardai would feel this way because he was dazzled by the graphics of the game, a reaction to a surprising leap in quality made possible by technological innovation that does not produce the same effect today. Screenshots of *Alone in the Dark* suggest as much, with its early polygon graphics making characters appear garish against the partially pre-rendered backgrounds of the house itself. The plot—a suicide with more at its core than originally suspected—is nothing we haven't seen at this point in time, though its execution is exceptional. The game sets up and deepens the mystery through atmosphere and aesthetics. But it seems important that Ardai didn't focus on any of that. Instead he said, "I feel that I have been inside a real house." The feel of the house, not the representation of it, was what was important in *Alone in the Dark*. In other words, it didn't matter if the house *looked* exactly right or if the figures were convincingly human or monstrous; what mattered was that the 3D space, paired with the sense of loneliness, made the horror *feel* real.

It's this feeling that activates the shared experience of horror, because it wasn't the monsters of *Alone in the Dark*, or the actual layout of the house, or even the mystery itself that impacted Ardai or future reviewers: it was the perception of being alone, in the dark, inside a real house. This kind of feeling requires a sort of mediation, a way for the player's mind to create the horror through interpretation. This labor is what cements the actual horror in *Alone in the Dark* and in most horror games that really work. The verisimilitude of the world that contains the terrors of the game is less important than a space that urges you to do the work to *feel* a sort of affective relationship toward it. And so the repeated plots in the *Alone in the Dark*, *Resident Evil*, and even *Silent Hill* series are less about bad writing and more about the sense of atmosphere being a highly personal interaction between player and game, which will be similar but not identical across experiences. As a result, the game's story matters far less than the story you produce through play.

The feeling of isolation is built upon in later games in the genre, specifically the *Resident Evil* series. Like *Alone in the Dark*, *Resi-*

dent Evil privileges puzzle solving, survival, and maximizing your chances of surviving a horde of monsters. Much like monsters, ghosts, and the supernatural were the antagonists for Edward Carnby and friends in the *Alone in the Dark* series, the depersonalized zombie is the antagonist for the team of special agents you control in the *Resident Evil* series. Both groups of antagonists in their respective game series require very little in terms of remembered plot to be effective, and neither represents a real human antagonist. Although human evil is apparent in both games, the memorable antagonists are inhuman, the things that stand as obstacles that cannot be understood or reasoned with and must be overcome, typically without a lot of help or ammunition.

The loneliness in both game series, then, hinges not simply on feeling like you are in a house by yourself but instead relies on an embodied feeling of loneliness. In other words, *Resident Evil* works because you feel (as Ardai felt in his review of *Alone in the Dark*) that *you* are alone in the manor where the game takes place, not your avatar. It's worth repeating: the scary part of these games is not their monsters or that the monsters appear to be real. Certainly, that helps. But the fear in these horror games is not premised on verisimilitude to ordinary life. The horror is in the design of these games, which elicits an affective response that makes you feel as if you are the one alone, hunted, and afraid.

* * *

The review space when *Resident Evil* came out in 1996 was a bit more bombastic than in 1992, not least of all due to the rise of next-generation competition between the Nintendo 64 and Sony Playstation. If the reviews of *Alone in the Dark* represented a sort of careful balance between consumer caution and journalistic access, the reviews of *Resident Evil* were more like the one Super Bowl commercial a local developer could afford: loud and flashy with a kernel of a message if you squint enough. *Computer and Video Games* had an eight-page spread on *Resident Evil*, complete with tips and tricks, clashing backgrounds, and lunging characters yelling gags like, "What *manor* of horror is this?!"[3] It's tremendously fun to look at, but as with *Alone in the Dark*, what the reviewers actually thought about the game was difficult to figure out. Luckily, the first sentence of the review, which seems to be written by a collection of unnamed staff, tells us all we need to know: "Perhaps when Capcom dreamed up the name for this game, they were trying to tell us something—that when you buy *Resident Evil*, it's as if a thing possessed has entered your home."[4]

It's fair to ignore the reactive reviews of the day that praised the graphics or panned the voice acting to focus on this particular element again: the impact of *Resident Evil* was that it *felt* like something had entered your home or mind and occupied it. The distinction between home and mind here is a bit less hard and fast than we might imagine, and that old cigar-smoking archetype of psychoanalysis himself Sigmund Freud claimed that the feeling we had when we saw something just-this-side-of-normal that made us feel just a bit off, isolated, out of place in the world was the experience of Unheimlich, or, strictly translated, "unhomelike." We typically call this feeling "uncanny," and both game series discussed so far employ this feeling to its greatest effect.

The enemies in this game are literally inhuman, but not so monstrous as to be unrecognizably human-esque—ghosts and zombies reflect our humanity back at us, though without recognition on their end. The setting is a home—albeit it far larger than your home—not in such disrepair as to be a ruin but declining enough to suggest that it accumulated dust and dead insects for thirty or forty years. If there is a feeling of dread inspired by each of these games that is linked to allowing a fearful thing inside your home or the feeling that you are in danger and alone, it begins at the ground floor, where you as a player respond. Once again, *Resident Evil* prompts the creation of fear in the same way *Alone in the Dark* did, and once again we see this amplified with a 3D space in which players move and, importantly, get lost. I won't claim technological advancement is responsible for aesthetic production, but the difference between rounding on a monster in a first-person 2D dungeon is profoundly different than rounding a corner in what feels like a real space.

And so *Resident Evil* is scary because it feels embodied, real. The subsequent titles in the series, *Resident Evil 2* and *3*, build upon this and introduce new sprawling settings. Yet, despite opening the world into cities, police stations, sprawling labs, and beyond, the game insists on tight corridors, limited supplies, and a crushing sense of loneliness. When there are other players who are part of your team, they are almost always elsewhere. When your character pieces together elements of a vast pharmaceutical conspiracy spearheaded by the Umbrella Corporation, the gathering of clues is done via scraps of paper, leftover diaries, traces left by the dead or people who are no longer there. Bodies do not unreasonably litter the streets, and the emptiness of the space outside of you and your unresponsive antagonists is what gives these games their sense of aestheticized fear: you are alone except when, paradoxically, a monster arrives, making you feel even *more* alone.

The plots of all three of the first *Resident Evil* games are fairly standard fare and mirror the *Alone in the Dark* model of unraveling a mystery, except with a bit more skullduggery and intrigue. The plots, crucially, are not important, and the conceit of the narrative in these games simply keeps you venturing farther into the blank, empty space at their center. Series that followed *Resident Evil* built upon this tension between narrative and aesthetic, between the intended effect and the bread crumbs of story that serve to get you there, in compelling ways. The *Silent Hill* series most famously leaned into the uncanny elements of *Resident Evil*, creating far more troubling and somehow more humanlike enemies for the protagonists to contend with as they enter the town of Silent Hill to look for someone they have lost. Regardless of how the games resolve—a claim that may aggrieve some *Silent Hill* fans—the ultimate impact is a sense of isolation in a town filled with nothing but unresponsive or aggressive mockeries of the human form. The covering of the face by bloody bandages, flaps of skin, or, in a particularly iconic example, a huge pyramid serves to emphasize this effect. You are looking for lost family members in Silent Hill, but nothing is looking back at you.

There are dozens of survival horror franchises of this era—loosely from 1992 (*Alone in the Dark*) to 2003 (*Silent Hill 3*)—that mirror this approach with varying degrees of novelty and insight. The *Siren* series plays with the idea of being able to see and hear what others can without being close enough to help. *Fatal Frame* shifts the focus of the mechanics of these games from the knife or gun to the camera. Capturing images of the inhuman things haunting you as a player creates a second level of remove, wherein your pictures further distance you from the monsters while also cementing their reality in your world. Even the very strange responses to *Resident Evil*'s massive popularity like *Dino Crisis*—a game in which players with limited supplies and ammo are on the run from dinosaurs—contain the same basic elements: enemies with some intelligence but no recognition of your humanity, which can in turn be recognized by you as not quite human.

* * *

It's remarkable that this aesthetic was successful through more than a decade of play, let alone that a sense of terror could impact anyone who played these games. It becomes perhaps less remarkable when considering the historical context in which these games were released, during what some would call the neoliberal boom of the 1990s, an era when, put succinctly, it was far easier to earn

money as a corporation while also distancing people from the social communities through which we share responsibility for our
fellow human beings. The gritty details are best left for someone
like David Harvey in his seminal *A Brief History of Neoliberalism*,
but here's an overview: Regulations on corporate spending had
been loosened during the twenty years leading up to the 1990s,
beginning with the moment that Paul Volcker, then treasury head,
said that the U.S. dollar would no longer be linked to the value of
gold. At this point, the dollar was effectively deregulated, and global trade was put under not the gold standard, but the dollar standard—far faster, easier, and riskier (well, risky for the poor). In the
end, neoliberalism hypercharged globalization and was instrumen-
tal in enforcing the conditions that have led to work being out-
sourced to poorly paid people working under dangerous conditions
abroad.

It also facilitated investments in the connective data networks
that define both global finance and the modern era of internet connectivity. In the 1990s, this connectivity was just beginning to become supercharged, with cheaper and preinstalled modem. The
U.S. economy was booming, allowing average people access to the
internet, and the world suddenly felt a lot bigger. But just as people
in major urban areas complain that they are lonely despite being
surrounded by millions of people, the internet era brought people
together without really increasing human connection. Human connection, of course, wasn't the point, and the internet served to
streamline not only business interests but the acquisition of knowledge and baseline communication, so it isn't as if we can paint it
with a broadly negative brush. But the feeling of being alone
among many was now relevant whether or not you rode the subway
with them daily. This fear of loneliness, nascent at the release of
Alone in the Dark and rampant at the release of *Resident Evil*,
fueled the sympathetic responses to the loneliness of these games.
In a moment of relative plenty, everything around us, from our

relationships to the environment itself, seemed to be crumbling or distancing itself from us. The internet had given us a community of people who were, at best, uncanny. And rampant business-first deregulatory practices had made the poor even poorer, disenfranchised, and forced to labor for the few who profited. Who wouldn't feel a bit lonely?

And then, suddenly, we weren't.

* * *

What happened next is too easy to describe incorrectly but too interconnected to get precisely right. We of course need to acknowledge that 9/11 fractured the American psyche badly enough to drive a sort of hyperaware surveillance mindset onto not only America, but most other first-world nations infected with paranoid delusions. This of course led to the Iraq War, an obvious-in-the-moment boondoggle and illegal war, and to conflicts that still rage in Afghanistan. There are better places to find full descriptions of this truly strange period in history—for instance, the excellent *Blowback* podcast—but suffice it to say that the sense of loyalty to Western idealism superceded the sense of global interconnection while maintaining a sure grip on deregulation and the increased profitability of massive corporations.

Perhaps this national fervor combined with a financial sector all too willing to issue bad loans to bolster an economy devastated by 9/11 and the George W. Bush administration, thus creating the 2008 economic collapse. This is the second event that changed us from a society that feared isolation to one that fears the monster. People who felt secure in their exceptionalism had been told they were not remotely exceptional twice: on 9/11, when they realized that others could attack them, and in 2008, when they realized that they too could face total collapse and homelessness due to the whims of bankers and financial gurus.

It's crucial to understand just how utterly defamiliarizing the 2000s were for Americans specifically, and globally to a large degree as well, as the global market cratered and American militarization was put into overdrive. Global changes like this don't happen in a vacuum, and the utter decontextualization and defamiliarization that followed in the wake of 9/11 directly influenced video game development, as it did every other kind of media. It is no coincidence that the horror genre had a bit of an identity crisis, too, and perhaps not surprising that the catalyst for change was the introduction of many, many guns.

Resident Evil 4, released in 2005, is the most remade and retooled game in recent memory. It was originally released for Nintendo Gamecube and nearly every console thereafter, including Nintendo Switch, Playstation 4, and Xbox One. A remake is in development for the next generation of consoles as well. This game has cast its shadow over fifteen years of gaming—a period of time that has witnessed the debut of many consoles that soon fell into obscurity—and it is still relevant. *Resident Evil 4* was also a risky departure from the *Resident Evil* formula, as it did away with the limited supplies that previous games relied upon as a way to add tension. Now, ammo and guns are relatively easy to come by, which posed a bit of a problem for the game; namely, if ammunition was no longer scarce, where did the risk that drove the gameplay loop come from? In other words, how could the game produce tension and risk for the player when a loaded gun made feeling alone far less scary?

This is a classic problem faced by the detective story as well: the introduction of the handgun throws off the balance, allowing anyone to kill at any given moment, without plan or feasible motive. Sherlock Holmes may have had to use his wits to gain access to the criminal mind in order to unpack the deep crenelations of the plots in Arthur Conan Doyle's classic tales, but there is a reason that the 1920s and 1930s saw the rise of the pulp, with Dashiell Hammett's

Continental Op and others preferring to shoot first and determine motive later. This is no great insight; it's something that writers and critics have grappled with for years, from Hammett's *Red Harvest* to Wes Craven's *Scream*. Introduce violence in an easy-to-obtain package, and the structure of the story you are telling changes dramatically, as any tension at an inescapable situation is potentially deflated with a quick draw and two shots.

For Capcom, the resolution was fairly simple: it introduced more enemies. *Resident Evil 4* is full of enemies, completely ignoring the ethos of the earlier games, which emphasized fewer encounters and more impactful moments of terror by extending the player's feelings of isolation. In *Resident Evil 4*, your character, Leon, is almost never alone, and not only because of the horde of zombies on the Spanish isle he has visited. The game is full of spoken parts, characters who act as secondary protagonists, villainous foils, and crafty merchants. With some, it's unclear if they have succumbed to the zombie plague, but what is clear is that they have recognized Leon as human, breaking the cycle of uncanniness.

And so the horror of the game is definitely muted; it's not entirely clear to me if *Resident Evil 4* is meant to be scary beyond a sort of existential fear surrounding a massive plague turning people into the walking dead. Instead, it feels like a game that is meant to be cathartic, allowing players the space to wipe out the enemies around them instead of fearing them from a distance. In this way, it is reminiscent of Sega's 1996 game *House of the Dead*, which spawned a number of sequels and stole many Japanese and American players' spare change at the arcade. *House of the Dead* is a shooter on rails, and if it's scary, it relies on jump scares and grossing players out; there is no loneliness nor feedback loop of fear. Instead, players are there to have fun and shoot zombies with a light gun, and the game succeeds admirably in producing this effect. The same can be said of *Resident Evil 4*, which isn't on rails— players can move their characters where they want and explore the island at their leisure—but is more shoot-'em-up than slow-burn suspense.

Perhaps the game clicked during a moment of hyper-televised violence and knee-jerk reactionary fervor. It doesn't have any recognizable politics, beyond heralding the end of the fear-of-loneliness genre. At the moment that the villains in *Resident Evil 4* looked back at Leon and recognized him as an enemy to kill, as opposed to simply following a sort of instinctive urge, the genre collapsed into something new. As the recognizing gaze of the villains in *Resident Evil 4* mirrored a sense of being suddenly seen and vulnerable, which rippled in the security state of post-9/11 America, it should come as no surprise that conceptualizing this new genre turn for *Resident Evil* would be as difficult as understanding the way securitization impacted our everyday life in the years following 9/11.

For *Resident Evil*, the search for a new identity would stumble over the same casual racism and intolerance that ran rampant during the Bush years, which materialized in, at the very least, some truly unfortunate optics. *Resident Evil 5* (2009) returned to the idea of hordes of enemies, but set the game in Africa, producing images of white protagonists gunning down dozens of black zombies. Developers of the game have long insisted that race is of course present but not meant to be derogatory in the game, citing the setting of the game as the reason for the predominance of black zombies.

Still, the game remains controversial, not least of which because it follows the historically racist and imperialist trope of white people "saving" Africa from itself. But the game still sold well, and the series continued with *Resident Evil 6*. This game was mostly forgotten, or at least passed over when discussing the series, and in this way, it is a lot like *Resident Evil 5*—however, the plot wisely avoided the white savior narrative and instead returned to its roots in the high-conspiracy genre, introducing more intrigue and twists and turns. For a game series that historically does not have much use for its plot, this largely went unnoticed, and the main takeaway from *Resident Evil 6* was that Capcom, the game's parent company, considered the series to be "bigger" than the survival horror market and that the games needed to adapt to the action genre. [5]

This was not an unfair statement in 2012 when the game was released. Through the Bush presidency and Barack Obama's first term, the games industry thrived on first- and third-person military shooters like *Call of Duty: Black Ops, Battlefield,* and even the curiously antimilitaristic *Spec Ops: The Line.* Action saturated the marketplace, and the sense of being alone had been jettisoned by the horror genre—in many ways, being crowded and overwhelmed by enemies was not only the trope of choice for games, but for politics in general. Fear of invasion, of replacement, drove mainstream politics for nearly a decade and arguably still drives it today, with Republicans like Pat Buchanan calling for border walls and the fear of terrorists lending popular support to John Ashcroft's notoriously vile Patriot Act. And standing as the sole guard against a breaking wave of enemies served to reflect these desires profitably for video game companies, which either did not believe their games were political or simply did not care.

But what then do we make of the horror genre, which requires the space for introspection to produce the sympathetic fear we described earlier? Loneliness isn't the only way that horror can be expressed or accessed, but nonstop action is not particularly scary in and of itself. No, the fear of being simply one of many, the fear of crowding, may have led to massive xenophobia, but it also is the core fear during the last twenty years of American culture. It just took until the middle of the 2010s for video games to recognize that fear and channel it into something beyond the reactionary lashing out at brown and black people.

Fear of isolation, through a long and painful journey during the beginning of the twenty-first century, had become a fear of never being alone again—a fear of no longer being the exception.

* * *

In 2017, Capcom released the seventh installment of *Resident Evil.* Seemingly a return to form, the game took place in a Faulknerian manor, crumbling and gothic, if also a bit contemporary, judging by the crud and mess infesting it. The game's trailer shows a first-person perspective, in which the character explores a series of locations, including a mobile home; a decrepit, refuse-filled house; and tunnels. Exposition flits across promotional sequences, but one of the most memorable qualities of the trailer is the appearance of the antagonist, a balding middle-aged man who is not exactly a zombie but can't be killed by multiple gunshots. "Dad is coming," a voice says, "we have to go now!"

At this point, the tone of the trailer changes, with a more frenetic shifting among points of view, including video camera shots of characters speaking who later appear as antagonists. A modernized remake of the John Jacques Rousseau folk song "Go Tell Aunt Rhody," sung by Jordan Reyne, begins at this point, and the lilting lyrics flit over the scenes of violence, terror, and pursuit. The synergy between the audio and visual is the second most striking feature of the trailer. The repeating lyric, "Go tell Aunt Rhody / Go tell Aunt Rhody / Go tell Aunt Rhody / Everyone is [dead]," is paired with a scene of the antagonizing family at a table filled with spoiled food, leering at the viewer, in a clear parallel to Tobe Hooper's seminal (and, I'll add, brilliant) 1974 film *The Texas Chainsaw Massacre*. The significance of pairing a folk song—one admittedly updated to something quite darker than the original version's dead goose—with this imagery suggests the lost innocence that characterizes the horror of isolation. We desire what we had when it is gone, and the sepia tone of the decaying house and the childlike melodies call back a sort of nostalgic defensiveness.

But the insistence on juxtaposing this nostalgia with the antagonists loudly and forcibly intruding upon your protagonist—leering and laughing, clearly in recognition of you as a peer, if one of lesser status—short-circuits this. Just as *The Texas Chainsaw Massacre* emphasizes the similarities between humankind and the animals that they ruthlessly slaughter in order to produce fear of the potentially dangerous people with whom we share our spaces, the *Resident Evil 7* trailer signals a sort of familiarity with the grime and cruelty we see that we can't just ignore. *Resident Evil 7* shows us no Leatherface, only the hitcher and the gas station attendant who seem harmless until they absolutely are not. Worse, the villains in *Resident Evil 7* appear, in the trailer, to not be entirely in control of their faculties but also not *inhuman*. That ambiguity forces us to question the humanity of our protagonist, too, and wonder exactly where the line between the real and the imagined horror lies in this game.

Unlike previous *Resident Evil* games, then, *RE7* is more complicated than the destruction of zombies and the fear of being alone. Indeed, although the plot follows the typically forgettable viral intrigue wherein the patriarch of the gothic plantation home we see in the trailer is creating a regenerative serum that infects people and causes violence (e.g., zombies of a different kind). The protagonist is called into the situation not as part of a paramilitary group, but as a husband searching for his missing wife. The lure of the personal recalls *Silent Hill*, but much like *Silent Hill*'s abortive but arresting reboot, *PT*, the unhomelike is replaced with a home that is overweaning and oppressive: hyper-homelike. Literary scholar Nicholas Brown has observed that when marriage is introduced into detective shows, they become sitcoms, which explains the lack of domestic drama in shows like *Dragnet*. In much the same way, the insistence on the lived-in home, even the occupied wreck of a home, shifts horror away from the terror of loneliness or isolation to the terror of crowding, of never being alone.

There are any number of games that parallel this kind of structure—and not as explicit or even implicit responses to *Resident Evil 7*. The 2019 co-op multiplayer game *The Blackout Club* plays with these issues in an homage to the 1980s teen adventure genre as a group of teens explores their town at night and avoids sleepwalking adults who potentially kidnap and kill kids in their strange fugues. The gameplay is not scary so much as collaborative and exciting, producing a cat-and-mouse chase that involves traps and clueless parents. But the introduction to the game is played alone and involves your character navigating its own home to try and escape a monster that can be seen only when you close your eyes. This combination of intentional obscurity that is required to see the threat coupled with the paradoxical sense of being surrounded by something unseen when you open your eyes imbues the home with a sense of deep menace. The dark of the house is deeper because the actual threat is living within the familiarity of the home and not simply an intruder in it. And if you escape the home, the threat exists outside of it in the people you interact with every day.

This latter complication may explain why so many recent horror games embrace the multiplayer genre; the familiarity both cuts and deepens the fear inherent in play. Games like 2016's *Dead by Daylight*—in which one player takes the role of a killer and five others, the flailing teen victims of an 1980s slasher, try to stop him or her—might speak to the potential of the multiplayer genre, but like 2013's *7 Days to Die* and 2015's *Dying Light*, the slasher-cum-zombie genre is reinvented as a sort of action movie, the fear replaced with an adrenaline spike. More typical of the multiplayer intensification of familiarity that we see in *The Blackout Club* is the unexpected hit of 2020, 2018's *Among Us*.

Although it isn't a horror game by any means on the surface, *Among Us* sets you on a spaceship with five to seven other players, one or two of whom are imposters intent on killing you and sabotaging your ship. Crewmates wander the ship, fulfilling certain arbitrary but easily completed tasks while they are stalked by people who look exactly like them. The crewmates can win by completing all of their tasks, or the imposters can win by killing off the crew or fatally sabotaging the ship. When players are killed, their bodies remain on the ship, and when others come upon them, they can call an emergency meeting, in which the living members of the crew debate who the imposters are. This of course means that the imposters are debating as well. A well-orchestrated game of *Among Us* always tilts in the direction of the crew, as players watch to see who is where, who is performing tasks correctly, and who is closest to a suddenly dead body.

But most games are not well orchestrated at all and devolve into the imposters telling obvious lies in often hilarious and ineffective efforts to create doubt, which causes crewmembers to accuse each other of being the imposter, which then leads to fewer and fewer non-imposters, as crewmembers vote them off the ship, casting them into space. The game is, you might be thinking, very similar to the grade-school game of Mafia (thanks to colleague Andrew Meyer for this observation). But *Among Us* differs because the game is set up over an internet connection and allows communication only when there is a meeting over a dead body. The tension and fear arise due to doubts and suspicions about the other players: everyone looks just like you, acts just like you, functions just like you—everyone is recognizably the same as you and shares your (cartoonish) humanity. You can't determine who to trust because you are performing monotonous, occupying tasks that make it difficult to pay attention to what the other players are doing. You are murdered while either emptying the trash chute or trying to do a card swipe, or you murder someone who is doing those tasks. The everyday quality of the horror in *Among Us* is precisely what makes it an often divisive and increasingly noisy and angry party game.

But it's unbelievably popular too! With millions of stream views, a Twitch smash hit, and a sudden piece of the zeitgeist, *Among Us* finds players crowded even when isolated by a pandemic in 2020. If Kitty Horrorshow's *Anatomy*—an indie horror game that perhaps captures the transition between the horror of the lonely and the horror of the many better than any major studio release— posits that "every house is haunted," then haunting is not a mark of inhumanity, but a mark of banal humanity. Every house is haunted, in *Anatomy*'s case, with a sense of being lived-in, of being occupied previously, of embodying some kind of materiality that its current occupants cannot touch or remove. As we have discovered in near-universal isolation during the coronavirus pandemic—depending, of course, on your government's commitment to safety— this unsettled quality of feeling surrounded by sedimented history is not limited to the home.

Indeed, although I can't cover every horror game released between 1992 and the present, the massive shifts in the trends of predominantly mainstream, AAA releases are fairly lockstep in their transitions. There's something to be said here about the gentle direction of history in these changes, by which I mean that the games themselves are not produced in response to history specifically—no one is releasing *Resident Evil 7* with, say, the murder of Eric Garner in mind—but rather that the games respond to the world in which they are produced. The sense of loneliness that occupied the minds of horror gamers in the mid-to-late 1990s was a mindset that assumed a certain tendency of history, an end even. Francis Fukuyama popularized this mindset with his influential *End of History*, a book claiming that after the fall of the Soviet Union, liberal democracy would lift all boats in its rising tide. Yet, even if we agree with Fukuyama that the world's political turbulence would end with the fall of the Soviet Union, then we are still left all alone together in the world, united but largely atomized. Or, at least, the predominantly wealthy, white, and privileged classes of people who were reviewing and playing these games (myself included).

The onset of 9/11 and the 2008 economic crash perhaps proved that history had not ended, that we were not alone in our shared acceptance of the American future, but it was the rise of the Black Lives Matter movement as a reaction to the murder of Michael Brown that caused people to again interrogate the history of American exceptionalism. Although this frame for thinking about horror games centers around the West—despite a predominance of Japanese games—the shift in mindset from the isolated fear of being alone to the overwhelming fear of being crowded is not American specifically. This is something that has occurred globally, particularly when the classes, races, and people for whom history has neglected speak back. It is no surprise that at a moment when we are forced to face the ugly materiality of the past in our homes, states, countries, and world, we begin to fear the presence of people instead of their absence. And as global warming continues apace, the sedimented quality of the past accrues, heightening this anxiety as it becomes existentially threatening to all.

In 2013's *Outlast*, a truly game-changing entry into the horror genre, you play as a reporter who breaks into an asylum on a random tip to find unexpected horrors. The actual content of the plot is, as usual with these games, not really the point—the point is that you are surrounded, unable to fight, and must rely on hiding yourself away or running from the monsters that pursue you. *Outlast*'s Steam Store page puts it more succinctly: "you are no fighter—if you want to survive the horrors of the asylum, your only chance is to run . . . or hide." This gameplay philosophy has been echoed in other massively successful horror games like *Alien: Isolation* and *Outlast 2*, and it parallels the agency given players in *Resident Evil 4*, which changed the genre. If you have a gun with a few bullets, you might be scared of the enemies these games throw at you; if you have a gun with a lot of bullets, you may find the experience more fun than terrifying; if you never had a gun to begin with, you lose all sense of self-definition and simply must survive as best you can.

At the turn of the 2020s, we find ourselves as a species faced with catastrophic climate collapse; centuries of sedimented tension due to immoral atrocities committed against various races, classes, genders, and nations; and a growing sense of doubt that we can ever even things out between the extremes of the few haves and the many have-nots. There may be action we can take, but how can we blame people if, during times of recreation, they take a small thrill from doing one thing that feels like the most obvious way out: run, hide, and try to survive.

2

FIRST-PERSON SHOOTERS

The Politics of Death and the Death of Politics

Video games are famous for being catalysts for blame: violent games have been fingered as culprits for everything from school shootings to teen suicide, and the political establishment often has shown a deep concern for censoring this violence in an effort to prevent it from spreading to the real world. But what violence gets prioritized in games and why? What violence is acceptable, and what violence is deemed too much? And if the ultimate aim of sanctioned violence in video games is to produce propaganda for state-sanctioned violence, then how can any violent video game be emancipatory or progressive instead of incendiary or propagandistic? As we see, the history of the first-person shooter genre is defined by this issue almost from its inception and cleaves closely to the historical tragedies that surround it. While the genre changes as it moves from the era of Columbine to the era of 9/11 and the war on terror, we also see how the social element of the game circumvents the more utilitarian aims of state-sanctioned video game violence and produces a rapturous, nonsensical free-for-all that is teeming with potential.

* * *

In August 2019, a video game YouTuber named Karl Jobst posted what charitably could be described as the most exciting video about the dullest possible subject. The video, called "A 20 Year Old DOOM Record Was Finally Broken,"[1] is an eighteen-minute, twenty-one second investigation of how a player named Midnight shaved off an extra second from the speed record for completing the first level of the 1993 classic *DOOM*. (Jobst himself is a speed-runner and gave the record a go but could manage only to get within a second of Midnight). You read that right: the video is an in-depth examination of how a speed-runner—a subset of gamer who tries to get the fastest possible completion time in games both old and new—was able to tear an extra second of completion time away from a game that, in 2019, was not only old enough to vote, but old enough to drink and rent a car. Surely you're thinking *this must be the worst use of eighteen minutes in the history of the world.*

You'd be wrong, though.

The video itself is a marvel, not least of all because Jobst is an impressive historian and documentarian and frames the record in the long durée of *DOOM*, from early attempts at code parsing to the discovery of speed hacks, to player-versus-player (PVP) competition and how that changed the speed game, and finally to the speed-runner community at large. The video is the kind of intro to gaming I aspire to create, both here and elsewhere, and is absolutely worth your time to watch.

The trick of the speed-run is fascinating, too, as it relies on a quirk in the coding of the game, which applies double movement speed when a player moves diagonally. This was discovered when players needed an extra boost in PVP matches and relies on the fact that simultaneously pressing two buttons on the keyboard (e.g., "left" and "up" to move diagonally left) produces a reiterative input for the game. Moving left and right (strafing) isn't quite as fast as moving forward and backward, so it isn't *exactly* double the speed, but it's a lot faster. And so the speed-run we see, the seven-second speed-run, which is the crown jewel of a well-known streamer and player called Midnight, is a madcap rush through the stage, the first-person perspective completely throwing off any sense of balance as the character rushes through enemy damage and toxic waste, ignoring the platforming the game wants him to perform, and reeling diagonally across a pixelated world. The timing—between the enemies, the doors one must open, and of course the precise button placement of the diagonal run—is incredibly precise. The run feels like a dance, choreographed and fragile, relying on the player following his cues perfectly, any mistake ruining the spell and causing the whole thing to come crashing down.

The funny thing about all of this is that the game itself, id Software's *DOOM*, is not known for its balletic qualities or its graceful fragility. It is a shame, but the precise movement, aim, and innovative thinking that captivated thousands of gamers and nurtured communities of amateur map builders and modders is too often overshadowed by the social fears around *DOOM*. And although we can in 2021 revel in Jobst's description of the soul of *DOOM*, we must also remember that this is the game that, along with *Wolfenstein 3D*, pioneered the first-person shooter (FPS) genre that has given parents, concerned educators, and TV pundits and politicians fits for decades now. The locus classicus for this fear is the Columbine school shooting in 1999, in which Eric Klebold and Dylan Harris murdered twelve students and one teacher before taking their own lives. The two shared a love of *DOOM*, and it was clear that their fantasies took a page from the game itself, as kill counts and the particular violent punch that the game hyper-emphasizes for its aesthetic informed their massacre. The less said about perpetrators the better, of course, though Dave Cullen's *Columbine* is a good place for anyone who is curious about the event without wanting to lionize the perpetrators. That said, the fact that these two boys loved shooting people in video games so much created a panic over FPS games, which influenced their development into the strange mélange of science fiction and militarism we see today.

But how the hyperviolence of *DOOM* gave way to the state-sanctioned violence of the massively popular *Call of Duty* series only to return to a strange coexistence during the last five years is not only a story about politics, but also a story about the way the internet was used to politicize and depoliticize the propagandistic elements of gaming.

*　*　*

There is no doubt that *DOOM* and its successors are violent and at times distressingly violent. There is something totemic and fetishis-tic about the weapons in these games. There is something unnerv-ingly satisfying about the act of killing that is enacted here. But there is also something aestheticized and divorced from real, mate-rialistic violence in these early FPS games that slowly vanishes as the world becomes more concerned with the proper moral trajecto-ry of violent urges. As we see, a political desire to push games into an acceptable realm of violence as opposed to acknowledging the aestheticized quality of that violence led to jingoistic celebrations of militarism that were undercut by the absurdity and sincerity of other players interacting in these games. Precisely how this hap-pens represents the story at the core of this chapter. This is the story of how the first-person shooter started as a goofy homage to hyper-violence, became a prop for U.S. militarism, and then somehow found its way back to its roots through the persistent stupid enthu-siasm of people who wanted to game with their friends.

*　*　*

Much like *Alone in the Dark*, it's difficult to find reviews of *DOOM* (1993) that aren't retrospectives. The game was as much a flashpoint for modern gaming as any other game in history, and it arguably influenced the medium for American gamers more than any other. As a result, there is a preponderance of retrospectives on *DOOM*, but not many contemporary reviews that are available without a robust archival search.

Still, for *DOOM* this is fitting. This was a game that spread via nonconventional means, from newsgroup posts to shareware kiosks in the local Staples in my case, along with many other cash-poor eight- to ten-year-olds. The way shareware worked—for those readers not currently knocking at the grim reaper's dusty door—is that you would buy an inexpensive floppy disc or, later, CD-ROM that contained a piece of a game on it. It was a bit like a demo disc before mass distribution and fast internet speeds made demos more plausible for modern releases. Shareware's origin in the early 1980s is generally linked to three men: Andrew Fluegelman, Jim Knopf, and Bob Wallace created software (inter-PC communication, database management, and word processing, respectively) that they wanted to market in new ways. Vacillating among "freeware," "user supported," and "shareware," the three men basically created the strange interstitial marketplace of free-but-not-without-strings software that we now know well as we search for, say, a flashlight or white noise app on our phones.

Such a breakthrough in the market was fairly staggering for 1982, and Wallace noted on an episode of the television show *Horizon*[2] that he came up with the idea through the influence of psychedelics (an early forbear of infamous drug-software conflationist John McAfee, perhaps). But fantastic origin stories aside, it's fair to describe the impact of shareware on the marketplace of early computer gaming as epochal: it leveled the playing field for distribution in a marketplace that, due to relatively less complex developmental tools, was already surprisingly level. This benefitted many companies, two of which we spend some time with here: id Software, producers of *DOOM*, and Apogee Software, which produced the raucous violence-and-attitude drenched *Duke Nukem 3D*. Furthermore, the two companies worked together to produce 1992's *Wolfenstein 3D*, generally considered to be the grandfather of the FPS genre, with John Carmack (who later helmed the development of *DOOM*) and Tom Hall of *Commander Keen* fame developing the game while Apogee published it. It perhaps says something about the small (if we're being friendly; incestuous if we're not) world of video game development that these two publishers were responsible for three of the most seminal FPS games in the genre, though id Software is the name most readily recognized for its development.

Wolfenstein 3D and *DOOM*, released just a year apart, relied on the buzz and word of mouth that shareware promised. To make the analysis about me for a moment (albeit a terrible mistake in almost every situation): I was too young to get into *Wolfenstein 3D*, though I'd heard the same rumors every kid had: violent Nazi killing, robotic Hitler, and so on. But *DOOM* hit a sweet spot: an early 1990s environment in which the prevalence of family computers meant a lot of households had a floppy drive available from which kids, aided by the laissez-faire parenting of an America on the cusp of a financial boom, mainlined violent video games their parents wouldn't necessarily approve of.

The catch about shareware, though, is that the game developers absolutely want you to buy the full game, too. And so for me and many other players, *DOOM* was limited to only the first third of the game, with an ending sequence that left you on a cliff-hanger: the main character, Doomguy, had to descend into Hell itself to fight his way back to Earth. *DOOM* provided so much action and gratuity at the outset that it wasn't really necessary to get more, not if you were too young or inexperienced to master the timing and patience needed in an FPS. Instead, the game existed, specterlike, on almost all of my friends' computers in its half-finished form.

For the older crowd who did enjoy the full experience, however, *DOOM* was a monolithic network-destroying beast, slowing and crippling university networks that hurriedly banned the game before students connecting over Netplay for multiplayer player-versus-player (PVP) ruined campus internet. The absolutely essential book *Masters of Doom*, which chronicles the history of the game, includes an excerpt describing the reception of the game at Microsoft headquarters as nearly religious; people reported spending sleepless nights playing *DOOM* with their friends. I could spend the entire chapter rehashing the cultural impact of the game hitting the adult gaming scene, particularly as concerns multiplayer, but the main takeaway is this: so popular was the game that widespread workplace and campus rules had to be put in place to save the network capacities of these early internet connections. Productivity was unsalvageable.

Of course, the game that was ruining workplace productivity and infrastructure wasn't *Tetris* or the nationalistic *Wolfenstein 3D*—it was a game in which an ultraviolent marine gleefully murdered demons on a satanic Mars. Pentagrams, blood and guts, and quippy lighthearted riffs on the life and death of people, zombies, and monsters were plentiful. id Software's loose sense of social propriety fueled this with an initial swastika-shaped level as a "tribute" to *Wolfenstein 3D*, which was later removed, as well as a difficulty selection screen that included the options (from easiest to hardest) "I'm Too Young to Die," "Hey, Not Too Rough," "Hurt Me Plenty," "Ultra-Violence," and "Nightmare." The first episode of *DOOM*, the one that my friends and I played again and again, was called "Knee-Deep in the Dead." The game did not shy away from the violent elements it presented and in fact reveled in them, which encouraged its famously robust mapmaking fanbase to continue the aesthetic of difficulty and gore in many self-made maps distributed free with id's blessing.

Of course, I'd be remiss in not mentioning the most infamous *DOOM* mapmaker, Eric Harris, one of the two boys who committed mass murder at Columbine High School in 1999. In a video he made, Harris claimed that the Columbine shooting would be just like *DOOM* and that the shotgun he had was straight out of the game. Harris's *DOOM* maps are rather typical entries in the genre, not particularly interesting in any way, which makes them troubling for parents searching for some sort of reason after the fact and even more tempting to blame the game. It's no surprise that six years after its release, *DOOM*, which had garnered a reputation as a fairly over-the-top game, was being hailed as the step too far that games had been trying to avoid since their inception. David Grossman, for *Accuracy in Media*, said the game was "a mass murder simulator,"[3] and the implicit fear that this simulation is what lead Klebold and Harris down the path to a violent reality set in quickly and solidified even more quickly.

Indeed, infamous lawyer-cum–culture warrior Jack Thompson had filed a suit in 1997 alleging that *Wolfenstein*, *DOOM*, and pornography had led to a different school shooting by a boy named Michael Carneal.[4] The suit sought $33 million in damages and was dismissed quickly, but the germ of the idea was there: the games that these kids all played were similar and must have impacted their behavior. The idea isn't totally out of left field, but—particularly in the case of *DOOM*—it ignores the massive popularity of the game in favor of a narrative that depicts it as somehow niche and dangerous. As I've intimated above, you'd be hard-pressed to find a kid who liked video games who *hadn't* played *DOOM* or *DOOM 2* by 1999.

Furthermore, the violence in *DOOM* and, particularly, in its successor from Apogee Software, *Duke Nukem 3D*, was sophomoric and rude but primarily drew from the tradition of the schlocky horror comedy of the early 1990s. *Duke Nukem 3D* lifts lines from Rowdy Roddy Piper's commanding role in John Carpenter's *They Live*, growling, "It's time to kick ass and chew bubble gum. And I'm all out of bubble gum." Meanwhile the aggressively goofy quality of the violence in *DOOM* recalls Sam Raimi's 1992 film *Army of Darkness* far more than Pier Paolo Pasolini's *Salò*. The jokes are often sexist, ableist, and in poor taste, but they are jokes you'd expect from the shock jocks of the early to mid-1990s, a period that gave us the warmed-over *Airplane!* retread of the *Scary Movie* franchise.

On the contrary, the blood and gore of *DOOM* as well as the satanic imagery therein was transformed by Klebold and Harris into something that was viewed as darker and with a clearly violent, antisocial intent. It is easy in 2021 to scoff at this and associate *DOOM*'s jokey schtick with the kind of eye-rolling apologia reserved for early 1990s comedy films. But in the moment, society was desperate for some sort of explanation for how two kids could snap and kill a dozen classmates. And the FPS genre, installed on untold numbers of school computers along with more refined successors such as *Quake*, was an easy target and indeed a specifically named influence on these school shootings.

* * *

If *DOOM* cocreator John Romero hadn't shot himself in the foot by claiming that his 2000 game and famous critical flop *Daikatana* was "going to make you [his] bitch" in wide-ranging ads in almost every video game publication, we might have a longer history of id Software fighting its new reputation as purveyors of murder, death, and aberrant social behavior. As it stands, the twin forces of *Daikatana* and the twelve-years-delayed *Duke Nukem Forever* made id Software and Apogee (now 3DRealms) afterthoughts throughout most of the 2000s. Although the impact of these games never abated—for *DOOM*, the fan community remains strong and now is able to play and trade their maps over far more stable and speedy connections—FPS games veer away from its schlocky and fun forebears in the year 2000 and beyond. Some games like *Painkiller* and *Blood*, not to mention console greats like *Goldeneye* and *Perfect Dark* for Nintendo 64, retained the basic genre premises of (1) first-person perspective and (2) gun held slightly above waist level, blasting anything that moved. And a series I talk about a bit in this and the next section, *Halo*, wore its influences on the early days of first-person shooters on its sleeve. But by the early 2000s, we were seeing fewer games like *DOOM* that dealt in the fantasia of ultraviolence and more games that tried to replicate the everyday violence of military encounters. The cultural tide had turned away from *DOOM*, controversy and all.

What is less clear is at what specific point that tide turned. It's plausible to say that post-Columbine, FPS games began to change the way they embodied violence, swapping out blood and guts for more nuanced or tactical encounters. Or perhaps 9/11 marked the turning point, since FPS games next evolved into the military shooters we now associate with the genre. Both dates are valid, though I'd caution against making a determination about the moment the FPS genre turned decisively toward militarism, since the nature of development cycles, not to mention the particular skew of history when viewed decades later, makes it hard to say anything for certain.

Suffice it to say that between 1999 and 2002, all of the most important and defining FPS series for the next decade released their first installments, and all of these games were pointedly *not* like *DOOM*. Part of this had to do with the rise of Sony's Playstation 2 and Microsoft's XBox and the way that they made 3D combat more aesthetically pleasing and more viable for multiplayer, the prioritization of which changed the mechanics and aesthetics of the genre. But a much larger part, I suspect, had to do with heightened concerns over the cartoonish and hyperviolent *DOOM* style of shooter, as well as a feeling of heightened paranoia and wounded American exceptionalism in the wake of 9/11.

The first of these series, at least, could have been motivated by the former, even if it missed 9/11 by the skin of its teeth: *Medal of Honor*, the highly realistic World War II military shooter, was released in October 1999. The war game genre was by no means new and had dominated the simulation game scene for years at this point. But there was something more action based and less tactical about *Medal of Honor* that was new; this was certainly a game marketed to the same history buffs who would play, for example, the Sid Meier simulations of historical sea battles in *Pirates!* but, simultaneously, the game found an audience in the same demographic of players that so enjoyed *DOOM* six years earlier. In his review for *Next Generation*, Jeff Lundrigan explains the success of the game, saying that "few things are more satisfying than shooting a Nazi in the face,"[5] and this more nationalistic reasoning certainly enabled the game to escape, for the most part, the intense scrutiny of moral groups after Columbine.

However, this deference to the non-*DOOM* FPS games should not be written off as time-and-place explanations. Even in its more recent iterations, the franchise has been a lightning rod for cultural panic. *DOOM* (2016)—a game discussed later—got this write-up in *Common Sense Media*, an infamous media guide for parents: "Creatures are not only blown apart, they're also torn apart by the hero. There's a steady stream of blood and gore, as well as lots of satanic imagery. Such curse words as 'f--k' and 's--t' are uttered by different characters. Our hero is also oddly abusive and needlessly smacks droids who've just handed him a weapon upgrade."[6] On the other hand, *Medal of Honor*'s 2010 release was reviewed with some hesitancy, as "an extremely realistic, intense, and violent military game that takes place in modern-day Afghanistan, a setting that might bother some families, particularly those with members currently enlisted in the armed forces."[7] The difference between *Common Sense Media*'s reviews here is subtle in terms of wording, but comes through clearly: *DOOM* (2016) is violent in the bad way; *Medal of Honor* (2010) is violent in the often troubling but ultimately necessary "good" way. Especially after Electronic Arts "recently took out the option to play as the Taliban in the online head-to-head mode."

The accolades heaped upon *Medal of Honor* (1999) rely on this equivocation, because a heralded game wherein the entire purpose is to make Swiss cheese of other human beings on a war-torn battlefield only can be heralded if it is also "necessary." A reminder of history—of how good it can feel to shoot a Nazi, if properly labeled as a Nazi, on a battlefield in 1944 in Normandy—is what the FPS genre needed to elude the third rail of Columbine. The mood in America after 9/11 certainly helped move this mindset along. *Battlefield 1942* (2002) and *Call of Duty* (2003) were both World War II FPS simulators that launched enormously popular franchises, both of which exist as of this writing. Meanwhile, Tom Clancy's incredibly popular *Rainbow Six* series continued apace for third-person games that could be brought in under the umbrella of "patriotically acceptable violence against others."

The reviews of these games once again tell the tale of the moment far better than I could and were possible only in their sedimented and entirely unself-conscious patriotic semiotics in the strange hyper-reactionary moment in America after 9/11. The editors of *Computer Games Magazine* ranked *Call of Duty* the sixth best computer game of 2003, saying, "This game ups the ante in the WWII shooter arena, and makes everything that has come before it seem as outdated as France's army."[8] The shot at France of course mirrored the then-current discourse surrounding its refusal to aid America's war against Iraq and the frequent legislation attempting to rename french fries "freedom fries." Meanwhile, *Battlefield:*

1942 was described by the same magazine, one year earlier, as "a near-perfect balance between fun and realism."⁹

It's important to take a moment here to pause before rushing through the greatest hits of these franchises, particularly *Call of Duty*, which has become one of the fabled "too big to fail" game franchises that define yearly release schedules. But the question that goes unasked in these reviews is, when did the idea of realism in these shooters become something to be desired? Jack Thompson, who attempted to link *DOOM* to school shootings, continued to castigate violent video games. But although he's attacked games like *Grand Theft Auto* or *Halo* or—the closest analogue to any of the patriotic FPS genre discussed here, the terrorists-versus-operatives fan-made success *Counter-Strike*—he seemingly does not worry overmuch about *Call of Duty* or *Battlefield* or *Medal of Honor*.

One of Thompson's most aggressive complaints against Rockstar Games's *Grand Theft Auto* franchise is that it allows you to kill police officers—virtually, *in a game that is not real*. He even has attempted to elicit the help of police officers in his quest against the franchise, albeit with limited support. That said, Thompson has a long history of pro-police litigation, even as the domino that tipped Ice-T and Body Count's termination from their contract agreement with their label Time-Warner Studios for their song "Cop Killer." And, just to make it clear that this whole police/military thing is a blind spot, this is a man who tried to ban an evangelical *Left Behind* game, saying the violence in the game was unacceptable due to its affiliation with Christianity. Thompson's targets are the outliers, the purposefully provocative, and yes, at times, the offensive or obscene. But those targets were *never* the military or the police.

Even as the *Call of Duty* franchise evolved to include more adult, contemporary themes such as torture or, in a recent release, the ability to drop white phosphorus on enemies, it received criticism from some players who argued that "the White Phosphorus killstreak perk . . . provides no context and does not effectively convey how horrible such a weapon is"[10] but was met with unconcerned silence from most everyone else. Meanwhile, the popular gaming press of the early 2000s, primarily gaming webcomics that had become enormously popular like Mike Krahulik and Jerry Holkins's *Penny Arcade* and Tim Buckley's *Ctrl+Alt+Del*, made Thompson a celebrity of sorts, producing comics that still get posted every so often in which the characters break the fourth wall and solemnly lecture Thompson on the fact that games do *not* make people violent and that gamers *are very good people, just do not push us any further, Mr. Thompson.*

It's all very earnest and silly, but there is something alarming about the lack of critical vision here. The goal, seemingly, is to refute Thompson's admittedly nonsensical attempts to tie real-world violence, in terms of an active causal relationship, to video games. In effect, though, Thompson's critics simply perform the same sort of essentialism, arguing that no representation of violence in a video game is bad. This has led to a blind spot that explains why we see no substantive critique of the war crimes and brutality of the mainstream FPS series of the moment. Even the critiques of *Halo* and *Counter-Strike* feel weak compared to the full-court press against the now-primitive-looking *DOOM*.

The defense of games by the Thompson critics essentially whitewashed any decision by any company in the future vis-à-vis violent or extreme representation. It is carte blanche to produce whatever content desired with the guarantee that the players of the games will not revolt against the games based on content alone but instead on some mixture of content and execution. In essence, it is the direct opposite impact of Thompson's attempted bans, and it obscures the more obvious blind spot that Thompson, gamers, and any of the morally outraged parent groups had regarding earlier FPS games: that if you include the military, *specifically the U.S.*

military, violence is not only sanctioned, but often considered solemn, necessary, even profound.

And if the more metaphorical sanctioning of military violence in video games doesn't resonate, consider that in 2002, the U.S. military released its *own* game, *America's Army,* which was literally and openly intended as a recruitment tool. Free to all, the game was, according to its own FAQ, meant to show "the whole world . . . how great the U.S. Army is." During an interview with *GameSpot,* Casey Wardynski, the officer who conceived of the game in 1999, says that he is "a research PhD. I run an analytic cell here at West Point and most of our analysis is on labor economics, and, for example, incentive structures."[11]

Wardynski doesn't see any real relevance between this specialization and the free game he has spearheaded that lets kids have fun with their friends and is licensed and controlled by the U.S. Army, so we can take him at his word, of course. *GameSpot,* for its part, pushes back on Wardynski almost not at all, the closest they come being: "Do you still come across the question that asks if there is a disconnect between the entertainment value of America's Army and the sometimes, maybe oftentimes, grim reality of the real-world battlefield?" Wardynski's answer? "You can't escape the central point, which is armies are built to employ force."[12]

Wardynski is right, of course, but this is meant to mesh with his argument that the game supports the "volunteer army" of the United States. Wardynski is a recruiter here first and foremost, and to paraphrase an old joke, the way you know that recruiters are lying is if you can see their lips moving. But the controversy around this game was limited to academics like David Nieborg who were appalled by the obvious propaganda of a free video game made by the army telling players what the "army is really like." Punk rock group Propaghandi included a song on its 2005 record *Potemkin City Limits* called "America's Army (Die Jugend Marschiert)" that critiqued the game by comparing Wardynski to a Hitler Youth spokesperson. Games artist Joseph DeLappe attempted to subvert the multiplayer in *America's Army* to critique the illegal war in Iraq by posting the names of soldiers and the dates they were killed in chat for a project called "dead-in-iraq." Based on the documentation on his website, the response to the project was one part bemused confusion and another part "lol."[13] Suffice it to say, *America's Army* did not receive the same opprobrium reserved for *DOOM* or *Grand Theft Auto*, despite being a literal attempt to encourage kids to create material death and destruction in an organization built to employ force.

In fact, Jerry Holkins of *Penny Arcade* said this about the franchise: "These *America's Army* games really seem to enrage some people. I have it under good authority that [my wife's] not crazy about them either. That's fine, you can all be wrong together."[14] This is, of course, the same Holkins who was so aggrieved by Jack Thompson's rage against games that he and his cocreator donated $10,000 to charity in order to show him up. Kudos for the donation, of course, but the inability to connect the fact that the army is banking on precisely the same logic that Thompson is in order to enlist kids helped to preserve the massive smokescreen that military shooters would provide for overt militarism and propaganda in the years to come.

* * *

The series that best encompasses the complex dance of propaganda-cum-consent is *Call of Duty*, the benchmark for military FPS during the last two decades and also the most acclaimed by both fans and critics of the military shooter genre. *Call of Duty* somehow managed to pair fairly rote jingoism with a sly sense of self-critique that can make critics do backflips to try and find a way the series is actually doing something politically progressive. The series weaves this balance with a shifting focus on games set in the past, present, and future, all with the central goal of creating a multilayered vision of U.S. Armed Forces that the now-ubiquitous Punisher skull symbol used by the police and military implies: that the military is made up of principled men and women who, due both to their own flaws and those of the world, are tragic and necessary heroes.

It's a powerful fantasy, and before delving into it, let me stop here and make something clear: *Call of Duty* is an incredibly fun series on the whole. There are more than twenty-four installments across several different console iterations, so there are highs and lows to be sure. No one, as far as I can tell, is about to ask you to pick up the version that came out for the Nintendo DS. But if we praise *DOOM* for the level of speed and strategy it brought to the FPS genre, then we need to credit *Call of Duty* for amplifying that, if also while standing on the shoulders of giants in the form of 1999's *Counter-Strike*. But the improvements to the first-person military shooter that *Call of Duty* produced—from the level of tactical skill to the quick-twitch reflexes, and even the interpersonal gamesmanship generated in its deathmatches—were profoundly important to the development of the genre.

Hopefully, we can critique the series while also praising its mechanics, because it's all too easy to pull a *Penny Arcade* here and wave away concerns about the *Call of Duty* series, particularly its single-player narratives, with effusive praise about the multiplayer and the mechanics. The game *is* mechanically compelling—some installments more than others, of course—and the story it tells *is* often gripping; these are, at their best, excellent games! But that's also the point. Recall *GameSpot*'s interview with Casey Wardynski. When asked what he thought *America's Army* did for gaming, he responded by explaining that "the major investment we are making, and we are proud of the payoff to gaming, is that the government did something that might not have happened in the industry for quite some time—and that's the database behind America's Army."[15]

Wardynski, when given a chance to offer a boilerplate answer ·
about the military's mission to help bring peace to the world via
gaming or some such, instead gives an answer that deals with an
actual gaming feature. Although the U.S. Army having a database
with your kill counts in it is, under any circumstance, distressing,
the upshot of Wardynski's surveillance here is a massive database
of stats to facilitate deathmatch tournaments. Surely the information in the database comes in handy, too, but it's at least sharing the
stage with an innovation that could be called a development in
gaming, which immediately gives Wardynski and the U.S. Armed
Forces a measure of credibility to the gaming press and its readers.

The point is this: in order to be good propaganda, the game must
first be a good game. It's all well and good to put out a military
shooter that is licensed and funded by the government, but—and I
imagine Wardynski has regression curves confirming this—if the
game isn't any good, it isn't going to work as propaganda. In order
to buy in, as the army needs its players to do, the game must be
good enough to warrant enthusiasm and excitement. It has to bring
players to the game day after day, produce a real emotional connection, and then use that connection to bring them to the army. It's not
much different than an advertisement, but on a national, militaristic
scale.

So if *Call of Duty* isn't good, it hardly makes useful propaganda.
And since *Call of Duty* isn't made by the U.S. government, it has
plausible deniability that *America's Army* does not. Infinity Ward,
the developer of most of the *Call of Duty* games of note, isn't
ostensibly or obviously owned or funded by the military or the
government. It's just a games studio with one major product that
makes an obscene amount of money by producing more-or-less
successful versions of that product. We absolutely can look at these
games and say, as we might of *James Bond* movies, that they're
about espionage or military intervention or colonialism, but they
have to be understood as works of art or popular fiction first and

analyzed as such if they are to be understood correctly. Their status as games made for entertainment, not recruitment, gives them cover to be jingoistic under a kind of interpretative, symbolic largess.

But the military, which often serves as advisers regarding weapon realism as well as tactical legitimacy for these games, signs off on them before they hit the shelves. Simon Parkin, in a 2014 article in the *Guardian*, is quick to point out that the association between games and the military-industrial complex is more symbolic than official. Indeed, he goes on, while film has the dubious honor of a history of CIA and government funding in its long durée, video games are more distanced from governmental influence. The government, Parkin tells us, has long advised games companies about *ideas* for games, and many successful games have crossed over into the world of military training, but the actual funding of games by the government as tools of explicit, purposeful propaganda isn't as easily codified.[16] Outside of *America's Army*, which uses the kind of barely hidden "subtext" that American propaganda typically thrives on—recall Holkins's defense of *America's Army*—whatever complicity exists between these shooters and the military is intentional, whether because the game developers want to use accurate guns or because they are chasing realism in their representations of war.

This latter desire, to make a "real" shooter, lets a sort of unified jingoism in through the back door. Take the tremendously popular *Call of Duty: Modern Warfare* series, which is often credited with a kind of subversive and critical point of view on American military tactics and exceptionalism. In particular, 2009's *Call of Duty: Modern Warfare 2* is cited by many as critical of militarism qua militarism due to its infamous "No Russian" mission. In "No Russian," you play as a CIA agent undercover with a Russian terrorist cell. In order to gain their trust, you join a mission wherein the group invades a Russian airport and opens fire on the civilians inside. You are given the option to join in the massacre or to simply watch it unfold, but regardless of your choice, the mission cannot be completed if you fire on your ostensible comrades in the terrorist cell. At the end of the mission, the terrorist leader turns on your character, revealing he knew all along that the player-character was CIA, and shoots him dead. This animates the Russian-U.S. conflict, which fuels the rest of the game.

Given the ink I've already spilled on *DOOM* (1993), I think it's fair to assume you, the reader, know how this level was received: moral panic, fears that kids would develop a taste for killing civilians, deep distaste and discomfort, and a small voice in the wilderness arguing that this particular level produced the kind of aesthetic and moral conflict needed for games to rise to the level of art. Jim Sterling, in an editorial for *Destructoid* prior to his ubiquitous YouTube gaming celebrity, argued the latter point this way:

> I hope [No Russian] gives players chills and maybe even makes them turn the computer off to think about what they just did. I hope, more than anything, that this debate will continue long after Modern Warfare 2 is released and we've finally played it, as gamers around the world ponder the necessity of what Infinity Ward did, and argue over its importance. If Modern Warfare 2 can do all that, then we can truly say that videogames are art. [17]

Much like the Jack Thompson tempest in a teapot controversy, it's worth noting for posterity that Sterling's strange insistence upon "games as art" in the final sentence is almost certainly a reference to film critic Roger Ebert's widely maligned claim in his 2005 review of the film adaptation of *DOOM* that "no one . . . has ever been able to cite a game worthy of comparison with the great dramatists, poets, filmmakers, novelists and composers." [18] This, of course, elicited disdain from gamers and games writers, webcomics, and so forth, and Ebert wrote several articles afterward both clarifying and doubling down on the claim. Obviously, my premise in this book relies on the idea that games could be art or at least aesthetically important, so I certainly have skin in this game, but I think Sterling's response to Ebert is emblematic of the value and necessity of Ebert's critique in the first place: a grasping attempt to crown something as art in order to defend a medium doesn't really count as a serious intellectual movement. We don't have enough pages here to document every triumphant journalist saying, "we've got that Roger Ebert fellow, games are art *now!*" but suffice it to say that each one took the basic structure of Sterling's comment here, wherein a critic observes a game giving a player a hard choice and citing it as proof of the concept that games are art. Crucially, though, the choice cannot contain the most difficult implications of the decision, and in Sterling's case, they are quick to note that "No Russian" does not say much about the violence it incites, but it does say a lot about how war breeds ambiguity:

> The easy thing to do is to take this information and view it as Infinity Ward condoning terrorism. However, I argue that such a point is dangerous to make. Just because we allow something to happen, that does not mean we condone it. America currently allows hate groups like God Hates Fags to preach against homosexuality and celebrate the deaths of American soldiers. Does this mean America therefore condones bigotry and hatred? Of course not. We all need to tolerate things in life. We don't need to approve.[19]

But I, and I think most art critics, would argue that art demands active choices and active judgments. Even art that is typically thrown under the bus as ambiguous, pointless, or subjective—like Jackson Pollock's abstract art ("My kid could do *that!*") or Donald Judd's massive sculptural installations that rely on audience reaction to give them meaning—typically intends to evoke a purpose and a reaction, which we as an audience can judge aesthetically. Indeed, art's ability to prompt judgment from an audience on its aesthetic success is perhaps the one unifying thread between most genres and media of art: Pollock's art says, "I am not Édouard Manet," just as clearly as Manet's art says, "I am not the kind of art that ignores the existence of a spectator." This kind of distinction looms especially large in film, where influence is so important and homage and pastiche defined the genre long before becoming hallmarks of contemporary and postmodern art. The auteur director says, "My work is like these directors and utterly unlike these directors," and whether or not we agree, we have to acknowledge the claim. In other words, we can always call bull on the art we encounter, argue that its positionality in the world of art or its claim to distinction is incorrect, but we have to acknowledge the claim's existence. Not so, apparently, in "No Russian."

In fact, I would say that if "No Russian" meant that Infinity Ward condoned terrorism, or, even better, argued that this kind of American action means that America is rotten at the core of its identity, then it would be a much better level and makes a case for being considered "art." I don't mean to pile on Jim Sterling, who certainly is one of the better and more astute journalists from the pre-2010s era of games journalism: although celebrating ambiguity is not something I can get behind, they are also right about "No Russian"—it is basically an acknowledgment that bad things happen from which we can't possibly draw any conclusions. Even the famous option that Infinity Ward added wherein players may skip the level without penalty does not, as *Rock, Paper, Shotgun*'s Kieron Gillen claims, make the artistic statement "bullshit." Instead it makes the level inessential. Gillen rightly points out in his article that the execution of the level leaves a lot to be desired but misses the mark when he argues that "it's not that the ideas are necessarily bad."[20] The ideas aren't necessarily bad *or* good because the ideas simply aren't *there*.

And if you're wondering whether this is a massive pot of ink to spill over a single *Call of Duty* mission and its relationship to art and politics, then let me add my own twist and explain that this is all a way to elaborate on what the main developer of the level, Mohammad Alavi, claimed that the level is supposed to do. Alavi, an Iranian American who, according to his extremely brief Wikipedia page, considers himself an Iranian at heart, did not have politics in mind when he proposed and developed this level. He was simply trying to make the Russia-U.S. war narrative of the larger *Call of Duty: Modern Warfare 2* make sense. Alavi said in a 2012 interview with *Magical Wasteland* that his primary goals when writing "No Russian" were to "[sell] why Russia would attack the U.S., make the player have an emotional connection to the bad guy Makarov, and do that in a memorable and engaging way."[21] In other words, the mission's purpose is expository. It's a story beat. The elements of terrorism and trauma were likely drawn from the air around him at the time of development, one would expect, as the 2009 release date was well in the shadow of the war on terror, 9/11, and the specter of everyday first-world terrorist violence. But it's nothing more than a set piece. The level did and does divide and shock people, and it certainly raised a compelling question—"No Russian" is worth talking about, no doubt at all. But there isn't much to say.

The story behind the level's skip option reveals a lot about the nature of *Call of Duty* game narratives as well. Alavi revealed in a conversation with *PC Gamer* that "an enlisted gentlemen [who playtested "No Russian"] immediately put down the controller and left the room. He said he wouldn't play that level. He would play the rest of the game, but not that level."[22] This is allegedly what made Alavi add the skip option, but it's a strange claim. The playtester, an active duty enlisted soldier, found the level in which white civilians are killed in an airport simply unplayable, disgusting, irreparably broken; however, the rest of the levels in which all sorts of other people are killed are totally fine. Pixels, as you might have said to Jack Thompson back in 2005, are pixels, after all. Why should it matter if they're representative of "good" targets instead of "bad" targets?

The reason of course is because the *Call of Duty* narratives are meant to position the military in a normative, banally heroic role. Even in "No Russian," your hapless protagonist is simply following orders that will enable him to further infiltrate the terrorist organization. The ends will justify the means, we imagine, because the military in these games has normal and intelligent and necessary plans, unlike what we so often see in real life. And if you're wondering whether I'm cherry-picking one game, one level even, we can return to Simon Parkin's *Guardian* article, specifically when he speaks to one of the main writers and producers from the early *Call of Duty* games, Dave Anthony. Anthony has a number of excellent quotes in this article that reinforce the strange invisible-but-pressing characterization of the military in the *Call of Duty* games. In the article's opening lines, he explains that six months after he left his job writing and producing *Call of Duty*, he got a job offer from the Pentagon, which wanted him to think about the future of war for them, and at the end of the article, he opines that he "would like to see more collaboration with the military and game developers." But perhaps most telling of all is this quote concerning his work on *Call of Duty: Black Ops 2*: "My greatest honour was to consult with Lieut. Col. Oliver North on the story of Black Ops 2. . . . I will never forget the stories he told me about the times he met former Panamanian dictator Manuel Noriega. There are so many small details we could never have known about if it wasn't for his involvement." Surely we all can agree that a disgraced former general responsible in large part for a massive scandal involving selling arms to terrorists is the person everyone would most value chatting with during games production.[23]

So although it is tempting to characterize the *Call of Duty* games as progressive or subversive when they seemingly critique the "any means necessary" quality of American militarism, it is important to step back and recognize that any critique in the games is superseded tenfold by the games' counterclaim that "any means necessary" is a good way to think about American militarism. Those who maintain this balance, this invisible assent, end up working on more *Call of Duty* games, as Anthony returned for the (very brief) storyline in *Call of Duty: Black Ops 4* in 2019. And those who are more interested in doing something else, like Alavi, end up going on to develop other interesting but not particularly artistically important games. Alavi moved on to help found the *Titanfall* team at Respawn Entertainment and worked on *Titanfall 2*, a game universally praised for its innovative, fun, and decidedly nonpolitical story mode.

The fun, fast-paced *Titanfall* games may do only what Alavi said he set out to do in "No Russian"—get the story going and involve the player—but they do this without a clear tie to military history or a potential military future. *Call of Duty* always keeps the future in mind, particularly the future *as it could be*; *Titanfall*, despite its more sci-fi roots, simply does not care about a plausible vision of the future. And although both games have in common a rabid multiplayer fanbase and a truly violent style of play bequeathed from their long-ago ancestors from the *DOOM* school, only *Titanfall*, particularly *Titanfall 2*, is consistently praised for the quality of its story mode, which is beloved for its innovative level design and condensed narrative. *Call of Duty*'s story mode is, typically, skippable, memorable only here and there. And perhaps it goes without saying that *Titanfall* allows the fun of the game to determine the story, whereas *Call of Duty* maintains a serious appeal to the logic and supremacy of U.S. militarism as a matter of course.

So is this stagnation in the most popular military shooter what is sending the narrative end of many expensive, top-flight—what industry people call triple-A or AAA—FPS releases into a three- to five-hour purgatory? Is the success of *Titanfall 2*'s five-hour narrative plus a robust multiplayer the reason that the industry is shifting to almost total multiplayer mode FPS games? Well, yes and no. It is true that people have become weary of *Call of Duty* story modes, but it's also true that *Titanfall 2* was not nearly as popular as it could have been. No, the reason we are seeing the slow death of FPS story modes is because the conditions under which they were introduced—an overweening security state that was galvanized by terrorism, retaliation, and war—are changing, if not ending. Games are responding to this change by recentering the player as they did during *DOOM* (1993).

In other words, for the first time in this book, we chart an artistic evolution that eliminated writing and narrative. The most recent and the best turn in FPS gaming has nothing to do with its writers and very little to do with the genre as art. What does it have to do with, you ask?

Plain, dumb fun.

* * *

In 2012, Rockstar Games—famous for its open world, outlaw adventures like *Grand Theft Auto* and *Red Dead Redemption*—published a game called *Spec Ops: The Line*. The game was an installment in a lesser-known tactical shooter series, and it was released a full ten years after its most recent predecessor, *Spec Ops: Airborne Commando*. The game, unsurprisingly, had little to do with this previous game or, in fact, any of the other *Spec Ops* games, which are standard military fare, simulating and celebrating the tactical situations and combat acumen of an idealized armed force. The first game, 1998's *Spec Ops: Rangers Lead the Way*, was essentially an advertisement for the Army Rangers and presented them as put-upon and deeply skilled heroes who had unimaginable jobs, a patriotic fantasy made in consultation with the U.S. Army Rangers. *Spec Ops: The Line*, on the other hand, was a story of three soldiers in the near future trying to stop a splinter group of murderous soldiers—the "Damned 33rd." Run by the war-crime-happy John Konrad, the group rounds up and kills citizens of a sandstorm-ruined Dubai. Your character is part of a three-man team, which is there to rescue, apprehend, or kill Konrad, depending on which part of the game you're playing.

In the end, though, you discover that Konrad had been dead for most of the game and that your main character—who has committed countless atrocities including the use of white phosphorus on civilian prisoners—was the only person who could hear "Konrad" and is responsible for his actions in Dubai, including the deaths of your two team members and countless civilians. In other words, the orders your character were given from command were delusions and the mission was nothing but a giant mistake, with no real purpose or predetermined outcome. The game relishes in this reveal, casting doubt on the mission through the narrative of the game and throwing up loading screens for the player that alternate between tips for playing the game and reassuring messages like "You are still a good person." The reveal shifts the plot away from a pro-American military adventure to a retelling of Joseph Conrad's *Heart of Darkness* or perhaps Francis Ford Coppola's *Apocalypse Now*. In all of these stories, a soldier attempts to retrieve a long-lost mentor only to find that the cruelty of colonialism and war has twisted that figure—Kurtz, Konrad—into a dark reflection of the world around them. And in the end, the person rescuing Kurtz or Konrad is also lost to that reflection.

The game, as you might have guessed, did not find a market and was a commercial failure. But on the heels of that failure, it gained a reputation as a game critical of U.S. intervention and from there amassed a cult following. If you talk to anyone about "smart" shooters, you'll inevitably hear about *Spec Ops: The Line* and possibly the feeling the "white phosphorus" scene produces specifically. The game is absolutely a master class in making players feel guilty about the actions they take, and it pulls off the more subversive elements of "No Russian" far more effectively because it clearly has some ideas that it is working hard to convey. Unfortunately, those ideas live and die with the idea that "killing civilians is wrong," an uncontroversial stance that helps explain why, even in such an antiwar war game, the military still serves as a rescuing force in the end.

It also helps to explain why the game—to minds of many the crown jewel of subversive military shooters—had such a minimal impact on the industry. In fact, seven years later in 2019, Infinity Ward released the most recent *Call of Duty* game, *Warzone*, and included the use of white phosphorus as a "killstreak reward" in the multiplayer. Although there was outcry and critique about the choice, we again see the type of critique characterized by the "No Russian" level: military types, in this case a former Marine named John Phipps in *IGN*, critiquing the lack of "realism" that would properly express the horror of using white phosphorus[24] and repeated reminders by journalists that white phosphorus is banned under the Geneva Convention. The significance of the inclusion from a moral, aesthetic, or thematic standpoint wasn't really at issue, in other words; instead the question was, "Is Infinity Ward really taking white phosphorus *seriously* enough?" A far cry from *Spec Ops: The Line*'s depiction of brutalized, burned bodies in the wake of an attack and seemingly a good example of the inefficacy of a critique of war that is embedded in the narratives of military shooters.

But the curious part about the inclusion of white phosphorus is the absolute lack of drama surrounding it after *Warzone*, the multiplayer that included it, came out. In fact, a quick Google search (December 29, 2020, for reference's sake) of "white phosphorus COD reddit" gets you an almost endless supply of comments saying that the white phosphorus killstreak reward is overrated, boring, and not effective in gameplay. It is, to use a gaming term, out of meta, which is to say that it can't be used to play the game at its highest level.

The fact that a political third rail like white phosphorus can be boiled down to a discussion of gameplay efficacy shouldn't come as much of a surprise, however, at least in terms of multiplayer gaming. When opened to a multiplayer space, games change in a way that can't be documented or proven very well at all outside of Twitch clips and highlights. What we see when we peek into that world is that gamers can be just as cruel and crude as advertised, with companies like Ubisoft trying desperately to softly censor slurs, obscenity, and discriminatory language in the chat space of its massively popular tactical FPS *Rainbow Six: Siege*. There isn't any denying that multiplayer spaces—particularly multiplayer FPS spaces as far back as *DOOM* (1993) and the incredibly popular but also incredibly toxic *Counter-Strike* and *Counter-Strike: Global Offensive* (or *CS:GO* as it's typically called)—aren't typically pleasant spaces, and the level of discourse in text or audio chat can be charted through any number of saved Xbox Live screenshots and Steam chat shares that I won't share here. For one, they are other peoples' experiences—outside of being yelled at here and there, I haven't had much experience with slurs—and for two, they don't really serve to prove any point. They are isolated moments of people behaving badly, and although any specific moment of cruelty should be met with full opprobrium, it's not as if we can legislate or prove anything about the social ills and virulent racism plaguing America based on the randomly firing synapses of angry gamers ages twelve to ninety-two online.

Perhaps we can turn to academia with Judith Butler's *Excitable Speech*, published in 1997 and blissfully unconcerned with video games, to help nail down why specifics won't avail us when it comes to understanding online interactions in FPS games. Of "injurious speech," Butler writes, "If language can sustain the body, it can also threaten its existence. Thus, the question of the specific ways that language threatens violence seems bound up with the primary dependency that any speaking being has by virtue of the interpellative or constitutive address of the Other."[25]

To decode this a bit, what Butler wants us to focus on when thinking about injurious speech is the fact that to make a slur or an insult specific enough to land, you need to imagine that it has a recipient ready and, if not willing, then predisposed to hear it. The "interpellative or constitutive address of the Other" can be restated then as "the ability of the other person on your chat, regardless of his or her specific identity, to hear, respond, and be impacted by your language." And although I disagree with some of Butler's more extravagant claims that stem from this one, I think she is absolutely correct when she argues that injurious speech requires some sort of imagined subject who can hear it and be injured by it. If I'm yelling slurs into my headset while I play *Halo*, there is someone listening who will get mad about those slurs, specifically someone on the other end who is probably not going to understand these slurs as reactionary or even as political speech.

Recall the reactions to Joseph DeLappe's "dead-in-iraq": he posted the names and life spans of dead U.S. soldiers in chat in *America's Army* and instead of angry political reactions, the responses were primarily variations on "huh?" or "lol." It isn't as if DeLappe was unclear in his politics or that the project was somehow misinterpreted by gamers not smart enough to get it: it's that the project of making gamers care about politics cannot be achieved in a player-versus-player (PVP) chat. In much the same way that *America's Army* failed to overwhelm military recruitment centers with enlistees, DeLappe's political project is drained of all political force without critique. The names and dates have no relevance to the contextual space of the PVP match, and they're not offensive or enlightening; they're just confusing.

As a result, the aggression of chat filters the impact of what is said: without an "other" who is willing to interpret and own the politics behind your insults, they end up as white noise. And white noise can hurt people, so it's a good thing that there are services that prevent players from making homophobic, racist, transphobic, sexist, or xenophobic remarks, because not everyone playing in multiplayer is going to be dulled to those words, and those words have an awful power to them. But that power is decidedly unpolitical in the sense of "global politics as concerns militarism."

Counter-Strike, the game that perhaps did more for modern FPS multiplayer than any before or after it, allows players to play as American armed forces or terrorists in a massive, violent game of capture the flag. Do players balk at playing either side, particularly the terrorists, since the game champions the sort of jingoism we see in *Call of Duty*? The only preference I've heard expressed is that the terrorists are the best side to play because they have the best guns. Again, the meta subsumes politics. Speed and lethality, as we saw earlier, defined the deathmatch in *DOOM* (1993), and the LAN or TV parties that followed games in that genre—from *Unreal Tournament* to *Quake 3* to *Halo*—kept people in groups of four to forty playing the same game under the same conditions, functionally draining them of any context other than which guns accomplish the arbitrary goals of the game best.

Rainbow Six: Siege and *Overwatch*, Blizzard Entertainment's hero shooter, are perhaps the franchises that employ this tendency of their players to depoliticize multiplayer spaces to the benefit of their own political and cultural cachet. Both add "diversity" to their cast by adding players of different ethnicities and sexual orientations. Both also conveniently shelve the strange and often xenophobic and reactionary backstories that inform both games. *Siege*, in particular, includes operators for use that have death's heads in their logos and employ torture as a special move. But any and all critique around these characters distills into a question of how effective the torture is from the standpoint of winning: if it is effective, then it'll be used, and if not, then it won't. As these games become professional with prize pools and teams that play them at the national level, the politics of the character choices are distilled into questions of efficiency and the metagame. Questions of morality are hardly entertained, let alone acted upon, which may ultimately disappoint Ubisoft and Blizzard, which cannot fully cash in their weak attempts at representative politics in their shooters.

But this evacuation of politics also includes the evacuation of the politics of shock. Although famously brutal fighting game series like *Mortal Kombat* can still make some parents nervous decades after its introduction, current shooters operate on a kind of accepted scale of violence. Most represent military incursions and are acceptable if they make the right mea culpas and meditations on violence and adhere to "realism" when using weapons of mass destruction. Games that do not include the military, on the other hand, have leaned into camp and nostalgia, birthing a whole new genre called the boomer shooter, which are FPS games that adhere to the old rules of *DOOM* (1993). For our purpose, it means that these games prioritize speed, lethality, and an excess of enemies. Games like *Dusk* and *Devil Daggers* emblematize this genre, as they present a panoply of light, sound, and input that can be shot at, bloodied, and razed at will. And their pixelated graphics keep the complaints about the violence low, and the veracity of the nostalgia high.

Finally, classic FPS series like *DOOM*, *Wolfenstein*, and *Serious Sam* are seeing resurgences, particularly the first two series, which have been rebooted to mass acclaim. *DOOM* (2016) is a boomer shooter at heart but also replete with blood, guts, and gore to the point of a sort of self-parody. *Wolfenstein: The New Order* and its sequel, *Wolfenstein: The New Colossus*, are both heavily political exercises in violence but have had crossover appeal to those receptive to its fairly liberal messages on race and history and those who find those messages irritating. Again, I could argue this makes these games less politically efficacious than their defenders might claim, but I think the important thing here is that the game has been celebrated for its gameplay despite the politics that are emergent, unclear, or otherwise.

Indeed, there's an argument to be made that these games, now slotted into a genre of their own and with expectations around violence that are normalized thanks to a self-referential sense of humor that they did not and could not possess in 1992 and 1993, have a better chance at becoming political than any other FPS games ever had. Here I will turn to Nicholas Brown and his "The Work of Art in the Age of Its Real Subsumption under Capital," which might make this argument clearer:

> even when the aestheticization of genre doesn't lead to an obviously attractive politics, it does lead to better art, or rather to the possibility of art as such—a possibility which, I have tried to show, today itself entails a minimal politics. A time-travel narrative can only have one of two endings: either history can be changed, or it can't: *Back to the Future* or *La Jetée*. So the problem of the time-travel flick is how to keep these two incompatible possibilities in play until the end, and if possible even beyond the end, so you can have a sequel. And James Cameron can, within this genre, make all kinds of intentional choices that can only be read as intentional choices, because they can only be understood as manipulations of a formal problem. And *Terminator II* can be a work of art, while *Avatar* is only an art commodity.[26]

What Brown is saying here is that the genre piece, the piece of art that has expected conditions that are consistently followed in order to succeed within its chosen genre, possesses a kind of clarity of purpose that lets politics in through the back door through intentional choices the artist can make after he or she has accomplished the conditions under which the medium or genre lives or dies. This possibility was not open to *DOOM* (1993) because the genre of the first-person shooter was being born as it was created, distributed, modded, and debated in the media. And at the same time, America's contemporary relationship with spectacular violence was being born, first through Columbine and then through 9/11. The liminal *becoming* of both of these things—the FPS genre and American violence via spectacular televised events—made guessing at genre impossible and wild speculation about the effects of violence in video games attractive. Now that the genre has stagnated and ossified, drained of politics, it has been transformed into a discussion of what does the most damage, when, and how, effectively making any debate about the shooters themselves a discussion of the metagame as opposed to the narrative on the page. With this transformation of the genre, the manipulation of genre has come in through the back door. A politics outside the military supremacy of the post-2001 shooter has been made possible by the total disinterest in these games' narratives—politics has found its way back to the FPS *because* its players steadfastly do not care about those politics at all.

*   *   *

Now, I wouldn't argue that we should designate *DOOM* (2016), *DOOM: Eternal,* or either current *Wolfenstein* as our most plausible art shooter. If indeed there are left-wing politics in any of these, they're on the surface, clear in the motion-captured replication of Jimi Hendrix telling your protagonist that he didn't want to fight in a war because the white man wouldn't fight for him. Solid politics! But also palatable, able to be shuffled through an AAA studio and into a wildly profitable multimillion-dollar project. That's interesting, but even if it is different in terms of political direction, it's not much different from what we saw in *Call of Duty,* at least in terms of type. It's narrative politics on the surface and obvious to the reader, and although there's a place for that, I'm not sure it rises to the strange shift in focus from the jingoism of the early 2000s to the political aporia of the present FPS games.

A game that comes closer is Kate Barrett's 2017 self-made game *Ready Player Fuck*. *RPF* is a send-up of both the first-person shooter genre as well as Ernest Cline's orgiastic pop culture fantasia *Ready Player One* (its sequel, *Ready Player Two*, was not yet released). Barrett creates a deadpan rendition of Cline's novel, a massive, polluted, and overbuilt world that is a backdrop for the protagonist's *real* world: a virtual reality (VR) headset. From there, the character interacts with every pop culture character that someone who was born between 1985 and 1992 and has a decent amount of disposable income could want, ending with a trip into space with a cute girl and Dr. Who.

If it isn't obvious that Barrett is skewering the pop culture nostalgia Cline curates, then the name of the protagonist—Zachary Knoxville Touchdown, "a nerd who lives in the stacks"—should provide a better sense of her intentions. Even more, when Barrett's protagonist says in the game's trailer that in VR "the limits of reality . . . are the limits of your imagination" before smash-cutting to Homer Simpson shooting X-wings, you get a sense that there's probably a critique of what counts as imagination here. Playing the game is an exercise in watching the parody grow and shift, satirically digging at video game tropes, manic pixie dream-girl stereotypes, and nerd culture.

But what makes *RPF* land so well is that the game feels like a typical FPS in so many ways. There are collectibles. There is a racing level that plays miserably on purpose. There are set pieces with giant monsters to kill. There are locked doors. There is a macho soundtrack and a mandate to destroy everything around you. The game obeys and fulfills the genre conventions it has to in order to work as an FPS, albeit a somewhat outré one, and once it has done that, it does more.

By "doing more," I mean that Barrett fills the whole of the world with a deluge of trite, silly, and meaningless references. Pop culture ties that make no sense fill the space of the game, existing next to each other for no other purpose than as a reference point and to make players who think they are above the critique the game is making embarrassed when they're suddenly cheering the giant robot level or getting excited to fly an X-wing around shooting at Bart Simpson. The game itself overloads its player with signifiers and gameplay mechanics and in doing so allows the excess to make its point for it. There is so much to see in *RPF*, but none of it is new. It is all rehashed, an imagination that begins to feel cloying and claustrophobic as your protagonist slowly gets the girl and whisks away in the Tardis as a job well done. You don't want to enjoy the pop culture in *RPF* even if you do; it's structural in that it structures a penned-in cage; it's exhaustive and exhausting.

Barrett's game imagines a simulation of the Cline novel that serves as a satire and parody simply through mimetic precision. It fulfills the conditions of the game so it is playable and legible and then forces the player to experience the humor and dread of an excess of banality. You could produce a game that is boring on purpose—*Penn and Teller's Desert Bus*, a true-to-life simulation of a hundreds-of-miles-long drive through the desert in real time, is an example of this—or one that produces a sort of biting media critique. However, *RPF* makes you not only critically consider the way that Cline's referential writing practice has infected art and media, but it also makes you complicit in it, experiencing and playing through it as an active participant and producing a remarkable and affective critique in the process. And ultimately we have to acknowledge that this kind of incisive critique would not be possible without the clarity of genre and emptying of politics that occurred over the long history of the FPS genre. In this way, we can see the long tail of video game genealogy produce art in surprising ways, just as we can envision the ways it could create something darker as well.

3

THE *SOULS* SERIES

Difficulty as a Way into Aesthetics—Aesthetics
Replaced by Difficulty

FromSoftware's *Dark Souls* series is known and beloved as a punishing and transformative gaming experience: a journey into the absolute limits of your own patience and perseverance as a gamer and a powerful aesthetic besides. The developers acknowledge it, as the *Dark Souls: Prepare to Die* edition's name suggests. Players line up for more challenges, deaths, and Pyrrhic victories. And that difficulty is heralded as the artistic flourish that makes this series not only enjoyable, but artistically important. But can difficulty be an aesthetic? Or does the series provide more than a sense of frustration and repetitive grinding to produce its aesthetic? In this chapter, I ask this question and try to solve an age-old gaming quandary: What makes the difficulty of hard games, particularly games like *Dark Souls* or *Pathologic 2*, so captivating? Are they more authentic? More true to themselves? To their players? Or is it something more akin to an artistic fidelity, and if so, how do these games matter when we talk about art and politics?

* * *

For my money, the most tedious current debate in video games is over "easy mode."

It isn't the worst debate in gaming, and it isn't the most annoying because it's being won by the wrong side. It's the most tedious debate because both sides make reasonable points so neither will ever win the argument. This is in part because each side is arguing for something slightly different, or at least materially different solutions to categorically different problems.

People who insist that all games should have "difficulty sliders"—customizable options that allow players to adjust the difficulty of the game from, for example, "very easy" to "very hard"—argue that these sliders represent access for gamers of different abilities. Gamers who might be differently abled or who simply are not practiced or skilled at fast Twitch gaming can use these difficulty settings to give themselves access to an experience they wouldn't otherwise have.

People who insist that difficulty sliders should not be in certain games argue that some games derive their sense of aesthetics and style, perhaps even their *meaning*, from the fact that they are painfully difficult by design and cannot be played otherwise. The idea, they argue, is that the games themselves tell a story that is only available via the medium of difficult gameplay; much like, say, Thomas Pynchon's *Gravity's Rainbow* or Jean Toomer's *Cane* would be different novels entirely without the extraordinarily dense signifiers their readers have to grapple with, these games wouldn't be the same, constitutively, without difficult gameplay.

And so the argument continues: access versus fidelity. The core of the debate seems to be about navigating who is allowed to experience these games, though from slightly different angles. Those who want difficulty sliders believe the games should be accessible to all in a very literal sense: they want games that anyone can play should they choose to do so. For these gamers, arbitrarily difficult games represent a barrier to entry. For the people who think game difficulty should be determined by the creator and not the player, the rejection of difficulty sliders introduces gateways to access for some players, but necessary gateways, since some content can't or shouldn't be enjoyed by everyone. The idea here is that difficult games don't resonate with some people because they are not meant to resonate with everyone, in the same way that difficult cinema or difficult literature may not resonate with everyone because it is intentionally alienating, difficult, or existential. In other words, the people who want difficulty sliders demand egalitarian access, whereas those who argue against them say that such access fundamentally changes the game such that the original intent of the developing team is lost.

When I tell you that the previous paragraphs are the most time I've spent on this debate, I am not lying to you, my friends. I truly have a hard time with this one, in part because two very persistent parts of my personality have stakes in both sides of this debate. These personality traits are perhaps best represented by the argument around this chapter's focus, the *Dark Souls* series, a beautiful and punishing game by Hidetaki Miyazaki and FromSoftware. Oliver Cragg represents one arm of my thinking and argues quite eloquently in the *International Business Times* that reducing the artistic intention of games to their difficulty "is the shadowed, all-encompassing crux that has often been used by critics such as the late Roger Ebert to deny the medium of any semblance of artistic or academic significance."[1] Adding an easy mode, Cragg suggests, would allow the artistry of *Dark Souls* to exist beyond the sense of difficulty alone. Erik Kain of *Forbes* represents the opposite perspective, arguing that it is "important to understand why the [*Souls*] games are challenging, not just that they're challenging. After all, it's absolutely true that what makes the *Souls* series great and memorable is much more than its level of difficulty. It's the way the world is designed, the unique aesthetic, the intricacy of its leveling and weapons systems, and the opacity of its lore and story."[2] And, like the proverbial two wolves in my brain, these two ideas kind of compete for dominance and create a mélange of "Well, I dunno. . . ."

Thankfully, one of my favorite games critics, Dia Lacina, wrote about this issue in an article on difficulty sliders in the game *Pathologic 2* for *Paste* magazine in a much smarter way than I could. She begins by distinguishing difficulty from accessibility, something that I conflated above because it is so often conflated within the discourse. But as Lacina notes, and as many disabled pro gamers would attest, the conflation itself both misses the point of how ability and difficulty function on different axes, it also is a condescending slip that falls back on the gamers who benefit from accessibility in the first place. Lacina explains:

> Difficulty is not synonymous with accessibility, which is the process of enabling as many players as possible to engage with a game, regardless of physical or cognitive ability. Color-blind options, subtitles, audio/visual cues, button mapping and the capability to adjust how button presses operate, and support for assistive technology are all accessibility options. They do not make the game less difficult.[3]

Accessibility, in other words, is not equivalent to ease, and although that seems obvious once it's said, it is so often missed in this debate that it may as well be ancient Greek. And so, since difficulty is not related to ease of access in Lacina's view, what is difficulty exactly? Lacina explains that difficulty "is the *subjective* experience of mechanical impediment, often in combination, to the player achieving their goals." The emphasis there is hers, but it may as well be mine, since the issue of subjectivity is the knife that cuts the Gordian knot of this problem for me, and I think for anyone concerned with artistic intention. Difficulty is absolutely a subjective issue, not an absolute one; if someone picks up the classic bullet-hell top-down arcade shooter *Ikaruga* without having experienced the genre, it will seem difficult to the point of inaccessibility. But if someone has spent time with these kinds of shooters before, the mechanics appear more familiar, the speed of the game makes more sense, and the experience is far less difficult.

Lacina ends her article with the explanation that "[difficulty] options, especially in conjunction with accessibility options, open games up for more players to experience them as developers intended, or on their own terms if they so choose," and she is absolutely correct as far as I can tell. Not least of all due to her point that fighting the battle of difficulty sliders in 2019, when she wrote the piece, is borderline quixotic, but because her analysis of subjectivity and intent gives due credit to both impulses. Yes, she agrees, if someone makes *Pathologic 2*, a game about surviving a pandemic in a town full of monsters and cruel, accusatory townsfolk, easier by using difficulty sliders, that might veer away from the developers' intentions. The game does derive its meaning from failure, and the player dying again and again in the world of *Pathologic 2* is a design feature, not a flaw, but this doesn't mean that the message of the game can't come through without that feature. It's also easy to forget that the developers themselves make these sliders and adjust the difficulty—there is intention here as well.

Most importantly, though, there are two things that Lacina's conclusion makes wonderfully clear to me. First, the relationship between intent and difficulty sliders has less in common with the rewriting of difficult work into SparkNotes and more in common with an index or footnotes added by editors after the fact. John Milton did not anticipate readers having indexed references to each biblical allusion in his work, and, yes, these allusions do change the tone and cadence of *Paradise Lost*. But we're all still able to glean his intention and his insights about the seductive quality of evil and the conflict of omnipresent foreknowledge and human frailty despite the change in the form of the work.

Second, if difficulty doesn't relate to artistic intention exactly—if hard games that are worth our time are equally legible when they are given a difficulty slider—then difficulty itself does not constitute an aesthetic. At least not a successful one. No one has accused the speeder stage in the 1991 *Battletoads* game for the Nintendo Entertainment System of being artistic, just infuriating. And yet "punishing" or "demoralizing" have come to stand in as aesthetic categories when discussing any number of important games in the last decade and change, be it *Pathologic* or, the subject of this chapter, *Dark Souls*.

It's diminishing to say that "the point is difficulty" with a game series like FromSoftware's *Dark Souls*. This is a whole world, crafted in a particular way, with a particular aesthetic, which has impacted millions of gamers over its life cycle from *Demon's Souls* to *Dark Souls 3*. But I've been guilty of describing these games this way, and many others have as well: the difficulty *is* the point, I would argue, and that means that reducing difficulty would diminish the value of *Dark Souls*. Ultimately, though, this is incurious thinking on my part; *Dark Souls* does cultivate frustration and difficulty, and that is a big part of the appeal of the series. But as Lacina notes, difficulty is subjective as is frustration; combat is part of the difficulty in *Dark Souls* and the lethality of the world is part of the frustration. But left at that, the games aren't special, they're just novelties.

Because an obsession with difficulty and storytelling has a way of privileging the former at the expense of the latter, the effects of this may help us glean what is so special about the *Dark Souls* series, why that special quality is so ephemeral and difficult to name, and what that has to do with the way we think about art and society at large.

* * *

In 2009, FromSoftware released *Demon's Souls* for Playstation 3, the first of what would become a defining series across numerous consoles. FromSoftware was not a fledgling studio by any means and had been responsible for the influential *King's Field* and *Armored Core* series, though the latter has been more financially successful for the company. *Demon's Souls* is popularly understood to be a spiritual successor to *King's Field*, though director Hidetaka Miyazaki has pushed back against such an interpretation. In reality, the medieval-esque setting and dark qualities recall *King's Field*, while the pace of fighting and intricate difficulty suggests FromSoftware's famed mech-fighting free-for-all, *Armored Core*. Moreover, like most games that draw from multiple forebears and influences, *Demon's Souls* is more than the sum of its parts, growing into something entirely different from the series that had made FromSoftware a success by 2009.

As we see through many of the games in the *Dark Souls* series, the history of their development, particularly in terms of what we can glean of Miyazaki's influence and intention, is muddy at best. This is particularly the case for *Dark Souls 2*, a fraught and polarizing game, which is most important to our purpose here. But *Demon's Souls*, as the first of the series, is a close second in terms of muddied waters: what part of its development is mythmaking by fans and by Miyazaki himself and what part is the actual history? In the mud of these games' origins, we begin to discover the secret to their appeal beyond their difficulty.

Demon's Souls's journey through development began like a lot of games in the late 2000s: as an attempt to resurrect an older genre of game into the current moment. We can see this in other chapters of this book—the return to survival horror in *Resident Evil 7*, the attempt to reimagine the computer role-playing game (CRPG) in Bethesda's *Fallout 3*, and the shift back to "boomer shooters" like *Dusk* in an attempt to recapture the magic of *DOOM* (1993). The idea of a finite or limited number of stories is not one that I put a lot of stock in; the people of 1708 were just as worried that there were no new stories to tell as the people of 2008, and we can see this in the slow, fraught birth of the novel. However, during certain moments in time, such fear causes creators to look backward to try and reclaim or recapture something that is no longer in the world because its own moment has come and gone. *Demon's Souls* was born of this impulse, as producer Takeshi Kaiji explained in an interview with *Edge*:[4] "I'm no fan of the genre Westerners refer to as the [Japanese role-playing game] JRPG," he begins, adding that "my desire was to revisit [a] lost area of gaming, to rediscover a charismatic corner of the medium."

Miyazaki builds on Kaiji's sense of excavation here, as he describes a game that pulls from media like books and film, a "dark fantasy" that made "the player feel rewarded for simply playing the game" rather than through a series of achievements or microquests. As the staff at *Edge Online* point out at the beginning of the interview, this impulse ran counter to the current vogue in games, and it caused players, according to Kaiji, to roundly reject the game during demos at Electronic Entertainment Expo (E3) prior to release. But Sony decided to let Miyazaki and FromSoftware continue along the path they'd begun.

What's fascinating about those players' reactions, though, is that they chart with general critiques of the *Souls* series: combat is too slow, too chunky, too unforgiving. A 3D action RPG, *Souls* pits you against strong and progressively more difficult monsters and monstrosities with swords, spears, knives, magic, and so on. Your defenses against these foes are the armor on your back and your shield, but much of the game involves precise dodging, backstabbing, and calculated retreats. Death results in the loss of a massive amount of progress, unless you return to the point of your demise to "reclaim your souls," a process that more often than not ends with a more permanent loss after dying along the way. From a design standpoint, critics argue that the palettes are gray and brown too often, the tone is too grim, there is too much about the game that discourages players from continuing.

As a result, setting aside the very reasonable claim from Kaiji that people "could never understand [*Demon's Souls's*] approach in five minutes," people saw the hallmarks of other video games they had played in the past and felt that the game didn't rise to its predecessors, much like other dark fantasy attempts (including the relatively polarizing *King's Field* series). Kaiji suggests that players were looking for more of a "musuo" game, a genre of game with a long history that's becoming more popular in America with the recent *Hyrule Warriors* series. The basic idea is that you play a single character beset by waves and waves of enemies that are relatively easy to kill individually but difficult in hordes: the *Dynasty Warriors* and *Earth Defense Force* series are two of my favorites. These games are a fun, fast-paced, and goofy power fantasy; they also are nothing like *Demon's Souls*, in which taking on two or three enemies at the same time usually means you are dead before you hit the ground.

Add to this the various penalties for dying, including losing character progression, health, and more, as well as a series of traps, hidden enemies, and environmental dangers that force hundreds of deaths for even the best players who play these games for the first time, and you can understand what Kaiji meant in his interview when he explains that the team were absolutely convinced "we went too far in this." *Demon's Souls's* director Miyazaki explains why this aesthetic is important to him, adding, "We really wanted players to focus on that part of the game, to feel the joy of having defeated challenges because they made the right choices. But to get to this point, you need failures, failures from which you learn." This issue of failure ties back into our difficulty discussion earlier, as well as Miyazaki's clarification of his view of the game: "It is not a game," he explains to *Edge Online*, "in which you die a lot, but an experience that keeps you very aware of your surroundings

and tests your knowledge of its contents and system constantly."
Kaiji adds that the game intends to "sidestep traditional narrative"
as well, something that would seem to fit neatly with an approach
to gameplay that privileges environmental and systemic storytelling.

It's understandable that so many approaches to this series take
the creators' words as their starting point, since Miyazaki and even
Kaiji are wonderful interviews, giving answers that seem concise
and clear. Miyazaki, Simon Parkin explains in an interview for the
Guardian, grew up very poor, unable to afford manga or popular
books despite a ravenous hunger for reading. He turned to the library, which had a number of English-language texts he only half-
understood at such a young age: "Often he'd reach passages of text
he couldn't understand, and so would allow his imagination to fill
in the blanks, using the accompanying illustrations. In this way, he
felt he was co-writing the fiction alongside its original author."5

In other words, Miyazaki, as the brains behind the *Souls* aesthetic at a directorial level at the very least, gained most of his own
aesthetic sense through interpretation and confusion, a sort of heur-
istic of inference as opposed to one of revelation. Much like paging
through a book you only half-understand while hoping the baroque
illustrations help convey something of the plot, the experience of
playing a *Souls* game is improved by being lost in translation. I
don't necessarily mean the literal translation from Japanese to English here—though, more than most games, the ambiguity immanent
to translation helps here more than it hurts—but the translation of
artistic explanation to artistic product. In other words, the *Souls*
games become too clean, too legible, if we take Miyazaki's word
regarding what they're supposed to do, because they are meant to
be objects of interpretation.

Attempts to pin down that ambiguity with explanations constructed from clues in and outside of the text to establish "lore" or a
consistent, unchanging plot may be satisfying but are also self-

defeating. The fact that there are no clear answers in these games is part of the reason they are so fun while being so difficult: the lack of ultimate satisfaction is an emblem of the *interpretative* difficulty that makes these games so memorable. The truth about the *Souls* games is that they are kind of chunky, strange, idiosyncratic, and inhospitable. They also are fun because of that inhospitality, not in spite of it. As Miyazaki says, these games aren't about dying a lot, but instead about being hyperaware of your surroundings, how strange and off-putting and compelling they are in spite of all of that. The difficulty then is not a matter of input functions or hair-trigger reflexes, but a difficulty of interpretation, an intellectual and aesthetic challenge that, crucially, does *not have a clear answer*.

Or at least it begins by having no answer. As we see here, the games change over time, and with change, they become more popular and players expect more of them. If Kaiji is correct in his assertion at the end of his 2010 interview with *Edge Online* that *Demon's Souls*'s "success and recognition is going to pave the way for other original titles to be developed and noticed," then the recent ossification of the "souls-like" genre seems to point the other way, toward a new style of expectation and sameness.

So how did we get here, and who got us here? As we discover, much like the initial boom of popularity that led to the success of *Demon's Souls* via word of mouth after initially disappointing sales, demands from fans for legibility and clarity about the lore and narrative of these games as well as choices by FromSoftware and Miyazaki to codify the story contributed to something different than the initial interpretive productivity present in *Demon's Souls*. How the series moves on from here is unclear, but those who it has influenced and impacted eventually will tell the story of what happens next.

But before all of that—or as a way of getting *to* all of that—let's step back from *Demon's Souls* the legend and take a closer look at *Demon's Souls* the game.

* * *

Dia Lacina has written elegantly about the *Souls* games, as well as about difficulty sliders, and I would be remiss not to return to her thinking on one of the more underexamined elements of this oft-examined series: the music of *Demon's Souls*.

Lacina's thoughts on the music help capture the slippery conceptual quality of the game itself. Discussing the music that opens the game, Lacina notes that *"Demon's Souls*, even at its most tranquil, is marked by peril. It's seared into the most delicately plucked harp. When strings flow smoothly, it is from a bow rosined with sadness and gloom. The Nexus is a place of respite. It is also a prison."[6] Indeed, the place where you find yourself at the beginning of the game—after your inevitable death in an unwinnable battle in the first level—is an area called the Nexus, where your soul returns every time you die. You are part of the world of Boletaria, never permitted to leave, but kept safe so long as you are among the somber denizens of the Nexus.

But as Lacina says, this safe space is also an *invitation* to peril, not simply an ambiguous prison/safe space. You have a goal in the game, as the fractured fairy tale of the opening narrative tells you: The king of Boletaria, Allant, has foolishly brought back ancient magic that at one point had destroyed almost everyone in Boletaria, and the city is now overrun by demons. Your job is to kill all those demons and bring their souls to the Nexus to gain power until you are able to kill (or, if you're feeling spicy, join) the Old One, the demon that is devouring the souls of the people of Boletaria and turning them hollow.

We see this plotline repeated in later *Souls* games, particularly the ending, in which the choices given the player boil down to "repeat the errors of the past" or "destroy the world as it stands," with no real sense of which choice actually betters the world of the game itself. Lacina puts this succinctly when she notes that the soundtrack parallels the game's own theses, asking the player "whether we do want to go on, what that even means, and who we even are in our transformed state."[7]

As the game meanders through five distinct areas—a sixth, marked by a shattered statue, is unavailable ostensibly because it simply was not completed during development—your character consumes souls to become human, die, and become hollow, repeating the process again and again. There is a sludge to the slog of *Demon's Souls*—rickety elevators, capacious asylums, choking sewers, castles guarded by hideous dragons, and wind-blasted cliffs with chromium skeletons and flying manta rays. But unlike the later *Souls* games, these areas are connected only thematically. They are their own distinct set pieces, and although I admire and appreciate the connected quality of the open world of the later *Souls* games, the confounding interpretative quality of the game shines in these discrete zones. Each is a kind of story told forgetfully, with a sense of recollection that does not quite get the point across fully but succeeds in conveying a feeling. There are storylines to follow about the king of Boletaria, about what happened to its citizens, about where the fat-faced cruel mayors of its cities now live, and about the human cost of Allant's terrible actions. But these storylines can be gleaned only from the voiced lines of dialogue from nonplayable characters and the descriptions of items in game menus, expository but abstracted and purposefully made vague and incomplete. The Lady of the Nexus is not about to pull your character aside and tell it what's going on here. In the sense that there is even a "here" at all.

In fact, most of what little groundedness *Demon's Souls* has for me as a player comes from the fact that I recognize elements from other *Souls* games in it. The mournful, depressed soldier who greets you morosely and sarcastically, *you'll never make it out of Boletaria just like everyone else who preceded you*, appears in some form or another in every game, ready to offer encouragement along the lines of, "Ah, another poor soul . . . be careful you don't turn hollow . . . ha ha ha ha ha ha." The name of this character, such that it is, is Crestfallen Warrior, and as in most games, you can talk to him as you play your game until he is simply gone, leaving "The Soul of a Storied Warrior" behind. No explanation is given for his death and just as crucially none is asked—you're left with his soul and one less person to converse with in the Nexus.

What's most compelling about the Crestfallen Warrior—and what has led many to (often misguidedly) compare the battles in *Dark Souls* to the battle with chronic depression and mental illness—is that he doesn't offer your character anything in *Demon's Souls* other than cynical mockery and vague advice about how to play the game. You could bypass him completely and lose nothing but another brick in the shattered totality of *Demon's Souls*. And that's part of what an interpretative as opposed to a narrative approach means: no single element is so important that it can't be skipped or passed over. The game expects players to miss things, to the point that some online guides are profoundly detailed, minutely ordered directions for making exactly the right moves to find a particular character in the Nexus or elsewhere. One way of understanding this difficulty is as a laissez-faire approach to the players, a lack of care about what they take from the game or whether they find it enjoyable. More interesting, however, is to understand the game as more than the sum of its parts, although the combined parts offer no more clarity to the game than its parts in isolation.

What *Demon's Souls* does best, then, is present players with a series of puzzles without satisfying answers and demands that they make the most out of those loose ends and confounding moments. The fact that it never wavers from this—that it never gives you a "good ending" or "secret room" that reveals the true lore behind all of the strange, stilted, cynical, and sinister characters you meet in your travels through Boletaria—is what makes this move work.

You're asked as the player to interpret and understand a world that is clearly and intentionally constructed but with all of the guidelines to that construction erased, showing only the finished product, a representation of an already ruined series of areas layered with their own silent histories. The stories you make about these places are born from your experience in the game—which may be why the multiplayer elements of the game, including player notes that provide tips (or lies), are so beloved—but the actuality of those stories remains out of reach, lost in a past you as a player or character were never able to see.

Somewhere there is a "real" story behind Boletaria, or rather there was at one point a story that filtered into *Demon's Souls*. The game is less a retelling of that story and more a palimpsest, a blank slate that retains the broad outlines of the story that was once there. The deep appeal of the game is that it is intended to be both a cohesive whole and an unremitting monolith, something that invites you in as a collaborator but keeps the answer to the world's order behind locked doors. Grappling and unpacking this is in itself an act of intellectual translation, one that mirrors Miyazaki's own story of childhood fantasy, and the deep resonance of this effort of translation is the reason *Demon's Souls* still has a hold over many imaginations twelve years after its release.

* * *

If *Demon's Souls* was the attempt at making something new that managed to get past those concerned with making a profit as Kaiji and Miyazaki suggest, then *Dark Souls*, the spiritual successor to *Demon's Souls*, was the first calculated guess that this new, strange genre might have legs. Miyazaki was again the director for the game but told Kadoman Otsuka in an interview for the book *Dark Souls: Design Works* that the game was going to feature an aesthetic that possessed "a certain kind of refinement, elegance, and dignity."[8] To that end, the set pieces in *Dark Souls* reflected the capacious asylum and ruined monastery/church of *Demon's Souls*, which was called the Archstone of the Tower Queen. The world in *Dark Souls*, much like that of its predecessor, relies not only on breadth but also on depth, a vast cosmology of up and down that creates one dizzying three-dimensional map reaching from the heights of a literal heaven to the depths of an even more literal hell.

The cohesion of this map is stunning, and the ability of *Dark Souls* to draw together vistas, which, within reason, contain vast expanses of areas you have or soon will visit, predated much of this kind of mechanic in open-world games. Many players were for the first time greeted with a world they could actively explore without arbitrary boundaries, thus tempering the question that haunted *Demon's Souls*: *Why do we explore the world?* We explore it because it is there to be explored. The value in the journey, that ephemeral thing that both Lacina and Miyazaki have observed to be the ultimate perplexity for players themselves, is given weight by the question of exploration. Figuring out what this world is and how it functions is a literalized goal in and of itself.

But much like *Demon's Souls*, *Dark Souls* doesn't provide all that much clarity about the world that you're so hoping to document and detail. The story is broader, involving four beings finding "Lord Souls" at the "First Flame" during the age of dragons. Your character, the Chosen Undead, must use these souls to alternately destroy the dragons and secret away the flame itself to produce the age of mankind, which has steeply declined following the sacrifice of one of the Lord Souls, Gwyn. Much like *Demon's Souls*, your character is asked to intervene in this problem after being killed in the first area of the game and at the end is given a fairly ambiguous set of outcomes: perpetuate the age of fire that has seen the decline and death of man or end it all and produce something terrifying, dark, and new.

The thesis of *Dark Souls*, then, seems to be much the same as *Demon's Souls*: you can't ever really understand the world entirely, but you still must make choices within it. It's important to note that the games are quite different from each other where it counts: for example, the aesthetics of the worlds they occupy. If *Demon's Souls* is a piecemeal set of stories, an anthology connected by the Nexus and a general tale about the world you inhabit, then *Dark Souls* is a novel cobbled around a frame story that links its worlds geographically and thematically. Your Nexus in this game is a bonfire where you wake up after your death and return to again and again, but unlike the baroque and filigreed Nexus, this spot is simply a place like many others, strangely verdant but surrounded by ruins and a number of paths that lead to death after death after death.

The distinction between these two modes of storytelling is made a bit clearer when we return to the aesthetic categories that Miyazaki tells Otsuka drove his team's process in making *Dark Souls*: elegance, refinement, and dignity. One reading suggests that this is normal video game adman-speak, a way of saying that *Dark Souls* sanded some of the many rough edges of *Demon's Souls*, but I think that gives Miyazaki and his team too little credit. No one's arguing that refinement, dignity, and elegance are *better* than the grime, ambiguity, and confusion of *Demon's Souls*, certainly not *Dark Souls* itself. *Dark Souls* is often a stunning picture of elegance, yes, but behind every veneer and filigree, the world itself is dead and dying. Gwyn's daughter, the bountiful and literally gigantic but beatific figure Gwynevere suggests that your character has found the promised land at the end of the punishing but gleaming gold Anor Londo. However, the figure of light you see is an illusion created by Gwindolyn, Gwyn's other child, who rules silently in the dark underneath of Anor Londo with the "help" of the false Gwynevere.

Behind every promise of light, plenty, and baroque satisfaction is the hard truth that the world you occupy is not dying but is already dead. The final fight in the game against Gwyn himself, the "Lord of Cinder" is accompanied by a soft piano score that contains as much menace as sadness in it. The battle involves your player killing what amounts to its heroic forebear, who is now hollowed, undead, and withered. Again, the filigree around the edges of *Dark Souls* intentionally chips and frays, showing the broken world underneath. If *Demon's Souls* is the exploration of a ruin that reveals nothing, then *Dark Souls* is the uncovering of a kind but poorly told lie about the goodness and coherence of the player's world.

As such, *Dark Souls* is, more than many games that get the moniker, a *spiritual* sequel to *Demon's Souls*, a return to the same questions of purpose, location, and totality posed in *Demon's Souls* but from a new aesthetic and narrative perspective. That the two stories come to the same end—with your character faced with the choice of perpetuating the decay of the world or ending it all for an uncertain future—lends the series a wonderful coherence. You're not asked at any point in *Dark Souls* to make sense of the stories you are given, and the cast of characters you meet is even broader and more impactful, and thus more ephemeral, strange, and reliant upon chance encounters. The rule of the piecemeal world, one that is not more than the sum of its parts because no sum can reasonably be made, persists in *Dark Souls*, a variation on a theme that rises to the level of its own song. To put it another way, when the Crestfallen Warrior reappears here, his warnings still as vague and cynical as before, he occupies the role of an archetype more than an individual, standing in for the game's Greek chorus or Shakespearian fool or horror movie omen.

But what does *Dark Souls* become when the archetypes are not variations on a theme, but instead specific characters recurring with their own long histories? The next iteration of *Dark Souls*—specifically its relatively negative reception from fans—sets the stage for a response that was detrimental to the aesthetic goals of the series.

* * *

Dark Souls II is polarizing.

Well, it's polarizing now, when you're reading this sentence. When it came out, *Dark Souls II* was less polarizing than maligned, at least by the standards of a *Souls* game. It received the requisite industry praise, with most outlets giving it a 9/10, and was a commercial and critical success. Where it was less successful, however, was among the player base that had made the first two games such hits. Perusing some of the immediate reactions at Metacritic—a site that collects and averages reviews, which has come under fire recently because its averages are used by studios to give or withhold bonuses to developers—we can see some critics break from the industry consensus to critique *Dark Souls II* for what they see as graphical mediocrity and tedious difficulty spikes.

We can also see that user reviews are split between "good-to-great" and "mediocre-to-awful." Most Metacritic users who like the game enjoy its atmosphere, its difficulty, and its return to the gameplay formula that we saw in the previous two games. Players who did not like it, however, cite poor mechanics in gameplay, tedious level design, and the fact that the game doesn't "add" anything to the *Souls* universe or blueprint. One user, Gamelore, had enough to say that it feels wrong not to quote the review verbatim: *Dark Souls II* "isn't failure due to a lack of resources. This is intentional failure injected into the game by decision makers (i.e., making it more 'accessible' to the much larger playerbase weened [*sic*] on post-16-bit games wanting fast content consumption, always-increasing 'progress' and no developed appreciation for RISK AND IMMERSION): In other words, SELLING OUT."[9]

This feeling of increasing access, letting new players in, speaks to the difficulty debate with which I opened this chapter, but it also relates to the perception of authenticity in the gaming world. A "true" game sequel relies upon a sense of continuity that often blurs into mimesis; the "authentic" *Souls* fan enjoys games that adhere to the formula of *Dark Souls* and *Demon's Souls*. Divergence from that formula, in terms of world building or storytelling or even enemy design, is seen as a kind of betrayal of the original player base, not least of all because of the punishing difficulty of the *Souls* series and the slow build to popularity it enjoyed through word of mouth. So the changes in *Dark Souls II*, particularly the way that fast travel is opened from the beginning of the game instead of painstakingly earned through death after death, are seen through the frame of compromise, the compromise to give new players access to the game at the expense of the fans who made the series what it is.

The problem, of course, is that the series became what it is by rejecting expectations in the first place, ostensibly at the risk of massive critical and market failure. Dozens of potential game series were smothered in the cradle due to a mix of ambition and obstinate divergence from the norm. Though some get remasters later on in life, like the strange and metatextual RPG *Moon*, rereleased on Nintendo Switch, they are perpetual what-if stories. But the potential of these games relies on the swings they take; no one wonders what could have been if a forgettable first-person shooter retread or a bumbling platformer would have been given its chance to shine. Ambition matters in the first iterations of these games; it is existentially important to series like *Souls*, which debut slowly and rely on an audience groundswell to build their legacy.

But when the original games have sequels, the players no longer want something new and ambitious: they want a repeat of the feeling they had playing the first game. As a result, every change, no matter how minor, feels like a slight or a concession, and *Dark*

Souls II made quite a few changes. Set now in the world of Drangleic, where "the flow of time is convoluted," you still control a version of the Chosen Undead who shifts between a human and a hollow form in a world slowly dying due to the overreach of the intellectual elite and aristocracy. In this way, Miyazaki follows the blueprint for *Dark Souls* carefully, but this world is also a new one. We do not get to revisit Lordran, the location of *Dark Souls*, and this new world is much more fantastical, like a fairy tale more than a dark version of an Arthurian legend. The color palette expands dramatically, and the enemies also multiply, though with some new spawning changes that vary the difficulty of the game.

But is it really the departure we saw in the comments above? *Dark Souls II* makes some quality-of-life changes and moves away from Lordran to another more fanciful Brothers-Grimm-esque world, but the game itself is still the deeply challenging model with identical leveling practices and the same essential mechanics behind them. For all of the ink spilled on *Dark Souls II*, the game is not particularly different from the previous two iterations in the *Souls* series. Its greatest sin is that it does not give its players an identical experience, that it tries to build on *Dark Souls* the way that *Dark Souls* built on *Demon's Souls*, presenting the same themes under different archetypal qualities.

Perhaps nothing better exemplifies fans' displeasure more than a seemingly benign elevator between zones. Like *Dark Souls*, *Dark Souls II* kept the interconnected world motif, allowing a sense of cohesion between zones connected by tunnels and doorways and elevators: down, straight, and upward. Though there is a three-dimensional quality to the games, verticality is the essential ingredient for their world building. So maybe it shouldn't be a surprise that an elevator on the top of an area called "Earthen Peak" that leads not to some kind of heavenly higher-than-high plane but to a castle called "Iron Keep" is such an incredibly potent flash point in *Dark Souls II*. The anger, confusion, and incredulous bargaining generated by this elevator can't be done justice in this chapter, since I don't want to quote dozens of people with usernames like "KomondorKeen666" explaining how this ruined the immersion of the game for them. But when I tell you that long articles on gaming sites like Fextralife called "Iron Keep: A Castle in the Clouds?" are just the tip of the iceberg, please trust me.

This 2014 article, which, curiously, is a defense of the legibility of the game's geography, reveals the core of the argument against *Dark Souls II* when its author, Skarekrow13, says that playing weeks' worth of *Dark Souls II* "led me to the conclusion that the Iron Keep location and elevator ride are not mistakes at all. Rather, they're likely clues made to illustrate world concepts."[10] The rest of the article is a detailed account of just how the elevator makes sense and the geography of *Dark Souls II* is actually quite legible, despite the mountains of critique it had garnered from the community. The actual details of that defense aren't relevant here—apologies to Skarekrow13—but the fact that the debate happened at all is fascinating.

It's fascinating because *Dark Souls II* tells us, up front, that time and other benchmarks of existence are "convoluted" in Drangleic. Dreamy transitions between areas, petrified wood that blocks paths and at times appears as people, and a long story that seems to wind through dream logic all suggest that any material logic here should be taken with a large grain of salt. Indeed, even the first scene, set in a small house with three witches, is so fantastical and different from previous and subsequent *Souls* games that its presence must indicate a lapse of material logic and an ascension into fairy-tale fantasia. And although this suspension of ground logic can be found in all of the *Souls* games, it is never as explicit as it is in *Dark Souls II*. So while gamers have attacked the lack of legibility in the game's geographical mapping, or defended it as legible, or argued, as YouTuber hbomberguy famously argued, that the mapping is important *despite* its critics because it speaks to the human condition more legibly than any of its predecessors, the game itself made its thesis painfully clear from the outset. The world in *Dark Souls II* has the interconnected feel of *Dark Souls*, but the connection is intentionally convoluted. The world is not supposed to make sense, and the game explicitly tells the player as much from the beginning. But this iteration of the archetypes drawn up in *Demon's Souls*—complete with the mysterious woman who gives the Chosen Undead power and the depressed soldier—were seen as aberrant, explicable only as an outgrowth of a studio that was appeasing new, less hearty fans with easier, more incentive-laden gameplay.

And so, just a few years after *Dark Souls* was rewarded for the divergence and growth of its series' themes, *Dark Souls II* was rejected by its most ardent fanbase for the same reason. There are critiques of *Dark Souls II*—muddy gameplay at times, meandering downloadable content, a repetitive endgame—but the game seems destined to live and die on the issue of whether it can be considered a proper *Souls* game or not. For a franchise that began by trying something deliberately new and unpopular just two games earlier, this was a monumental shift.

* * *

In the aftermath of *Dark Souls II*, surely some gamers must have wanted a quick return to the *Dark Souls* experience they thought they missed out on in its ostensibly direct sequel. But what they would get again was another departure, to another world entirely, not Arthurian or Brothers Grimm inspired, but more like a dark, Lovecraftian London filled with the omnipresence of beasts, blood, and a sense of all-encompassing celestial doom. *Bloodborne*, FromSoftware's next game, is not technically a *Souls* game—if you pay extremely close attention, you can see it doesn't have *Souls* in the title. However, two of the more invested *Bloodborne* critics, Sophie Pilbeam and Sinclair Lore of the evocatively titled Snack

Covenant, argue that the game is a refigured *Demon's Souls II*. The game has several layers, some procedurally generated, and peeling them back and tying it to the type of lore in *Dark Souls* has become a favorite pastime of players.

But is *Bloodborne* really *like* the *Souls* games? Well, yes and no. The death mechanic—in which you can reclaim your experience points if you can reach your bloodstain before dying—stays largely the same, and the basic look and mechanical feel of the game is very similar. But the setting is wholly different, with more city areas, libraries, churches, and the like. Although these are not unheard of in other *Souls* games, the lack of open fields, vistas, and the lonely expanse (outside of one truly distressing beach) makes the game feel Dickensian or, at most, like the blasted heath of a Brontë novel. Furthermore, the combat is faster, without shields—a standard aide against constant punishment in *Souls* games—and now with guns, which help your character perform the parry mechanic that is necessary to survive Yharnum, the setting of *Bloodborne*. The nature of the game itself is enough like a *Souls* game to tempt the imagination and make the connection for players but not so close that it requires mimetic representation of the past games to land correctly. And Miyazaki and FromSoftware run with this.

At this point, we are two games in without much commentary from Miyazaki or his colleagues at From. The reason for this is largely because I don't trust their commentary much after *Dark Souls*. I don't mean to suggest that any of them are lying or misrepresenting the game; in fact, the interview with Parkin cited earlier occurred after the release of *Bloodborne*, and it is a fantastic read, incisive and compelling with a clear sense of self-awareness. But after *Dark Souls*, the language describing the game—difficult, punishing, rewarding after time, hard-core, and so forth—was ossified into the discourse surrounding the series. Even *Dark Souls II* was judged primarily on whether it truly *was* punishing and ruthless or whether it was "accessible." The PC release of *Dark Souls* was subtitled "Prepare to Die Edition"—the game's marketing terms colored any media access irreparably. Miyazaki's standard discourse around mystification, translation, and access are at work here, as they were in previous games, to produce something special and aesthetically compelling. But the actual narrative about what these games ought to provide their players is set, and that's a powerful detractor when it comes to "industry interviews."

But one thing that shines some light on the shift from Drangleic to Yharnum is what Miyazaki's collaborator says about his approach to the monsters he embraces as enemies in his work. In an article for *Killscreen*, Gareth Martin quotes Masanori Waragai, one of the art designers for *Bloodborne*, from an interview he did for the book *Dark Souls: Design Works*. Waragai tells the story about designing the undead dragon in *Dark Souls* and how his first design, "swarming with maggots" and relying on "gross-out imagery," irked Miyazaki. "Can't you instead," Miyazaki reportedly told him, "try to convey the deep sorrow of a magnificent beast doomed to a slow and possibly endless descent into ruin?"[11] This speaks to the aesthetics discussed earlier, particularly in the more distressing, less aesthetically or narratively totalized worlds of the *Souls* games, but it is perhaps most revealing when we see *Bloodborne* as a culmination of this desire. The beasts in Yharnum are cosmic, yes, but unlike the gibbering fear of a Lovecraftian terror, these monsters are tragic, former humans turned into bestial terrors that are all the more terrifying due to the glimmers of their humanity that yet remain.

The character that most represents this in thegame is one of the most notorious bosses, Father Gascoigne, a hunter like you who has descended into bestiality. The lore in *Bloodborne* is, like in the *Souls* games, fragmented enough to be almost a matter of subjective interpretation, but it's clear from his garb and his (initial) humanity that Gascoigne is more like you than, say, the werewolves or hulking zombies. Still, his voiced lines tell a tale of temptation and acquiescence, and he greets you by saying "beasts all over the shop. . . . You'll be one of them soon enough." As much as this may sound like the Crestfallen Warrior from the *Souls* games, Gascoigne is not content to cynically chide your miserable fate, but in fact indulges in the corruptive blood, the sickness that has infested the world of *Bloodborne* and that your strangely garbed plague-doctor-cum-executioner must weed out. "What's that smell?" Gascoigne asks as he transforms from man to beast halfway through the boss fight you have with him. "The sweet blood, oh, it sings to me. It's enough to make a man sick!" For Gascoigne, sickness is to be desired in order to relinquish his painful existence for a bestial one, an existence he predicts will befall your character as well.

In this sense, Gascoigne represents the enemies of the game in total, from the meager mobs to the monstrous sinewy beasts to the strange hunter who first helps you to grow stronger but later turns on you if you take a particular path, becoming an incredibly strong enemy. All of these characters desire the return of health, but if health is in as short supply as we see in Yharnum, then acquiescence to a transformative sickness is just as good. The tragedy there is that many of the more important enemies in the game chose sickness, embraced bestiality, and rejected their humanity. In a *Souls* game, this marks a new iteration on the themes we saw in *Demon's*, *Dark Souls*, and *Dark Souls II*—this is not living in decay, but living in an active crisis, watching the world burn around you instead of watching it be snuffed out. And, in the end, you still can make the choice to rebuild the world you know or to create a new one; you still are tasked with impossible work that leads to no noble resolution. But *Bloodborne* takes a step laterally, asking what a *Souls* game would be like if, instead of being the Chosen Undead who is sent to save a damned world, you are the Crestfallen Warrior, asked to put out the fires around you when everything is terrifying, physically and emotionally.

The tragedy of a mighty beast in an eternity of decay exists in *Dark Souls*, both figuratively and literally in the character of the Undead Dragon. But the question of how that decay is tragic and not simply sad or pitiable is only acknowledged and engaged in *Bloodborne*, making it the riskiest and the most successful variation on the *Souls* theme: a fully changed vision of the world we found in *Demon's Souls* that is, paradoxically, familiar. A variation on a theme.

But though *Bloodborne* refused to answer the aesthetic and narrative questions the *Souls* games asked, fan response to *Dark Souls II* ultimately forced the series to come to a "conclusion," which ultimately demonstrated the necessity for this ambiguity and the consequences when it's eliminated.

* * *

When the trailer for *Dark Souls III* was released, it was immediately clear that FromSoftware was trying to return to a past product. The idea of linking the fires, kindling the ashes of the world, and bringing flame back to the world took center stage in a way that it had not in nearly a decade. This was not *Dark Souls II* and the strange, twisting world of Drangleic nor the fallen world of Yharnum and *Bloodborne*. It wasn't even the claustrophobic trap of Boletaria. This was a return to the world of *Dark Souls*.

And I specifically say that rather than "Lordran" because, technically, *Dark Souls III* takes place in a world called Lothric that charitably could be called Not-Lordran. Your character has failed to become a lord of cinder and so must gather the powerful lords together as the "unkindled," producing a new age of fire or a new age of dark in the end by the force of your own decision. If you're experiencing déjà vu, that's natural: not only does this game contain an almost literal continuation of the plot of *Dark Souls*, it even has some of the same nonplayable characters, including a play on the incredibly popular Siegmeyer of Catarina, Siegward of Catarina, bedecked in the self-same onion armor that made the former, slumped against a wall waiting for something to happen in *Dark Souls*, so memorable. The game truly feels like FromSoftware decided to listen to the fans and play the hits.

Of course, there are plausible reasons for this: *Dark Souls III* features the return of Miyazaki, who had delegated some duties to others for *Dark Souls II*. The return to high fantasy from *Bloodborne* may have pushed him back to his old, comfortable design mindset. But none of that feels like a good explanation as to why we have a return for the first time in five games. The *Souls* series is built on ephemerality and ambiguity, a sense of not quite being able to put your finger on what is happening and why, and particularly of not being able to name your own agency within it. In *Dark Souls III*, the connection to the other series and the callbacks are comforting reminders, references we as players of the series are meant to get and be rewarded with, as opposed to discomfiting aberrations in the wilderness.

In this sense, the aesthetic project of *Dark Souls III* seems to me to be more of a revision of *Dark Souls II* than a new entry in the series; the oft-cited fact that it is the "conclusion" to the *Souls* games speaks to this fact, as the series itself acts as a group of loose anthological stories as opposed to a complete narrative, at least until *Dark Souls III*. The gameplay itself is quite good, beautiful even, with areas that provoke awe. But the story feels too functional by half, a product of fan criticism that *Dark Souls II* wasn't enough like its predecessor and a desire to create an appropriate "end" to a story that was intended to produce feelings of dissatisfaction.

If we use Miyazaki's own design notes, we might say that if *Dark Souls* is the Undead Dragon as that majestic enemy comes to fruition, ruined and tragic with a sense of a long history that will never be revealed, then *Dark Souls III* is that same dragon drawn to scale in an anatomical model, given fully fleshed-out characteristics, and pinned to the table. In other words, if the other *Souls* games simply show us the barren world and let us put together the pieces, *Dark Souls III* intervenes to say, "no, here's how this all goes together correctly to make sense."

Not to dwell on this any longer than necessary, *Dark Souls III* is FromSoftware and Miyazaki's reaction to the dissatisfaction their fans felt with *Dark Souls II* and its deviation from the expected return of the world of Lordran. This need to produce fan satisfaction, something that was totally at odds with the way that *Demon's Souls* began the franchise, informs why this game feels both deeply unsatisfying and perfectly suitable as a conclusion for the *Souls* franchise. Left at the end of a series of games that produce and create, we have the ashes of the world trying to be reborn or simply die—a perfunctory nod to a kind of continuity that does not really make sense in the aesthetic of the world—and then darkness.

In short, if we imagine the fire keepers as a metaphorical creative spark leading from the dusty beginnings of *Demon's Souls* to the charred embers trying to be blown into sparks of *Dark Souls III*, the concept of aesthetic burnout seems apt. Because continuity—the need to provide some sort of answer or satisfaction to an audience—goes against the creative urge that we saw bloom in *Demon's Souls*, such that it brings an end to the creative process that produced these games entirely.

Dark Souls III snuffed the fire, for better or worse.

* * *

Perhaps the only conversation that is historically less edifying than the difficulty slider controversy I opened with is the discussion about authenticity in gaming. But we're going to bravely wade in anyway, sword and shield aloft.

I touched on authenticity with *Dark Souls II*, but I think it has even more relevance when discussing the current output from FromSoftware. The company continues to release games like *Sekiro: Shadows Die Twice* and the upcoming *Elden Ring*, both of which have been more or less relegated to the "*Souls*-like" genre that has taken over the gaming world. Which of these games is most like a *Souls* game and why is it the topic of exhaustive and, often enough, *exhausting* conversation. The series that began by rejecting any sort of conventional path or inspiration has produced a discourse around its games that relies on a codification of their qualities into a particular genre. And woe betide those games that do not deliver on this generic promise.

But in the case of *Sekiro*, a game that takes place in feudal Japan and relies on stealth and quick reflexes, you can see From and Miyazaki trying to make a new path forward. One boss battle in *Sekiro* has your character suddenly fighting against a knight in full armor who is trying to find his (seemingly dead) son. You fight this armored monstrosity on a bridge and eventually succeed in knocking him through the wood planks of the bridge to his death. More than one person has noted the similarity between the standard promotional figure for *Dark Souls*, the depressive knight in armor, to the boss in *Sekiro*, and more than one person has suggested that the boss battle entails an attempt by Miyazaki and From to part ways with the *Souls* games, to make an attempt at a clean break.

But the fact is that with the amount of money there is in *Souls* games, the rabid fanbase, and the massive expectations for every FromSoftware release, the freedom that the creative minds behind *Demon's Souls* once felt is unlikely to occur again. That aesthetic triumph of ambiguity, despair, and dead ends that we see in the *Souls* series is unlikely to bloom again from the same field, despite the quality and beauty of *Sekiro*.

And so when gamers see images and video from the Bluepoint Studios remake of *Demon's Souls* for Playstation 5, some are excited by how good the game looks and feels now, and others are frustrated by the lack of authenticity. The game, they say, does not *feel* like *Demon's Souls*; it's too clean, too polished, too much like a modern game. And I hasten to say that they're totally right, but their complaints are less about wanting the same experience they had playing the game than they are about feeling the same sense of potential, of intentional aesthetic foreclosure, of difficulty in the sense of interpretation.

There's a scene in "Bart Sells His Soul," the fourth episode of season 7 of *The Simpsons* in which Moe Szyslak, the crusty owner of Moe's Tavern, considers converting his bar into a family restaurant because "nobody likes hanging out in a dank pit no more." Homer's friend and drinking buddy Carl, panicked, asks Moe, "You ain't thinking of getting rid of the dank, Moe?" When Moe responds that he might, Carl responds, "But Moe, the dank . . . the dank!" For Carl, the misery of Moe's is also the heart of Moe's, and it isn't simply a single kind of misery, but a patina, a dank overlay that determines the appeal of the tavern. This is, I think, what players mean when they say that the remake of *Demon's Souls* is too "clean" or too "polished": the game is missing the patina of experimentation, of clumsiness, and of earnest attempts to create something unseen.

And though the reiterations on the themes throughout the *Souls* series produce this feeling in more and less successful ways, the commedia dell'arte quality of the *Souls* series cannot survive *Dark Souls III*'s attempt to codify the archetypes into singular, repeating, and continuous characters. And so the fire goes out, able to be reproduced but never really relit in the modern moment.

Don't cry for Miyazaki, From, or the *Souls* games, though—that patina, that effort of creation, that *dank* remains as a part of these games, enjoyed by many and understood by few, if any, by design. The games remain ready to challenge, to surprise, and to frustrate, all in the interest of telling a story about the self and the world that may not be pleasant, that may even be difficult, but that is worth telling.

4

METAL GEAR SOLID

No Heroes Left, Send in the Heroes

The *Metal Gear* game series, particularly the *Metal Gear Solid* set of games, lives in the shadow of its massively popular, almost legendary director-cum-auteur Hideo Kojima. A series about a flawed special operative named Solid Snake who is betrayed and disillusioned at every turn, *Metal Gear* tackles issues of nuclear proliferation, for-profit soldiers of fortune, and scientific overreach, all while analyzing the impossibility of finding heroes in the mess of war and statecraft. But over time, and thanks to a prevailing market interest in finding a star to sell these games, both Solid Snake and Kojima himself have become the centralized focus of the series, turning games that were once criticisms of "great man theory" into exercises in it. How can we explain this trajectory, and what can we take from these games, which remain incisive and compelling pieces of art, even as they drift from their original focus? As we see, the making of a hero for the marketplace is incompatible with a series that rejects heroes. But this doesn't mean that the market-friendly installations of *Metal Gear* are uninteresting—indeed, they set the stage for the deconstruction of the series and the auteurism of Kojima writ large.

* * *

It's hard to talk to people about the *Metal Gear* games.

Well, scratch that. It's easy to get people to talk about the *Metal Gear* games: easy to get them to describe how they felt sneaking around as superspy Solid Snake; easy to get them to opine on their favorite and their least favorite games in the series; easy to get them to think about the arc of the series, its origins on the Nintendo Entertainment System, its peaks and valleys along Playstations 1, 2, 3, and 4, where it succeeded and where it slipped up; easy to get them to praise the work of director, writer, and aspiring auteur Hideo Kojima and critique the shortsightedness of the Konami corporation for cutting ties with him. In short, it's easy to get people talking about their fandom of the game series and why it is so important to them personally. And as we've established time and again, this is no small thing. But *Metal Gear* has risen to the level of hagiography, the kind of game that only ever gets discussed in terms of pure positivity or the few things in the series that mar the overall brilliance. And as a result, it's hard to get people to talk, to *really* talk, about *Metal Gear*.

In this way, Kojima has become the auteur he clearly has aspired to be, particularly during the last decade or so. As anyone who wants to talk about Akira Kurosawa or Stanley Kubrick knows full well, any conversation first needs to surmount the barrier of its topic. The great directors—the auteurs who seemingly control every element of their production and combine a Herculean effort into a single intention—all require their due before discussion can turn to the actual work itself. Take David Fincher's commentary on Orson Welles, in which he archly suggested that *Citizen Kane* was as much the work of the cinematographer, Greg Toland, as it was the director, Orson Welles. This isn't a surprise to fans of the film, since Toland's name appears almost as centrally as Welles's in the opening credits, but the controversy stoked the argument regarding where true credit lay for that crown jewel of American cinema, *Citizen Kane*: Is it the vision of the director or the technical work of those working the cameras that confers genius?

But beyond Toland and Welles, beyond the ex post facto argument over credit and who deserves it, the film exists as a piece of art that has more than enough to say. And yet none of the plentiful themes the film tackles is really considered in this controversy; the hubris of the great man seen in Kane himself is reflected in both Fincher and Welles's strange egotism, and Kane's regret after wasting his life on ambition is a far more potent flash point for contemporary American culture than who the *real* genius was. And yet, the question about genius demands to be fully answered before a single frame of the film itself—not to mention Welles's and Toland's many *other* wonderful films—can be considered.

This is the problem with great person theory, the idea that oversized and brilliant personalities create and determine culture, almost separate from the actual materials they produce. Although we certainly acknowledge those who are involved in the collaborative process of building the massive projects that games and films represent, there's an epistemological or knowledge-based issue produced by this logic. The great director is only a great director after his or her first major defining film, after all, and usually more. However, after canonization, the director's work becomes a protected class of art, important and seminal not only *before* one watches it, but without even the necessary step of watching it. And at this point, debates about the aesthetics of film or, in our case, video games take a backseat to the debates about the personalities themselves. "Never mind what the long, continuous shot in *Touch of Evil* might represent or say to an audience," a critic might now say, "it is enough that Welles is behind it, so let's start there."

So we start at a disadvantage with *Metal Gear* off the bat, simply because it is part of the sacrosanct Kojima catalog. Even compelling, quirky games that were not received with the kind of unified zeal as his later games—strange early gems like *Policenauts* and *Snatcher*—have been canonized retroactively as pieces of game history, warts and all. And that isn't to say, as with Welles, that there is no reason for this—Kojima is a fabulous storyteller and a visionary game creator. He is also, it must be said, one part of the massive machine of games creation, particularly when it comes to his most acclaimed work, the *Metal Gear Solid* series. However, he should not be deified as an unblemished auteur who creates only hits for those who can recognize them: Kojima's work ranges in quality just like anyone else's. Indeed, much of the challenge of reading his work in the *Metal Gear* series is acknowledging the distinctions among the games and understanding them not as a monolith but as a series of, yes, uneven efforts.

As a result, I won't present as much from contemporary reviews here. *Metal Gear*, more than any series covered in this book, entered the zeitgeist with the release of *Metal Gear Solid*, and finding a review or an interview about these games that isn't part of the mythology is nearly impossible. And this is a problem for a game series that, for at least the first four entries of its massive output, is committed to demythologizing the heroic and the concept of the "hero soldier" and the "good war."

In an attempt to understand what this demythologizing effort entails and how it progresses once we stop thinking of *Metal Gear* as art and instead as a monolithic achievement and genealogy of the game's central figure of Snake, I take a step-by-step approach. I consider the first four games closely before turning to a reading of the rest of the series as a particular choice in response to an audience demand for a heroic through line, a demand for a message from the games that was edifying and reassuring in its vision of the world as one defined by exceptional individuals.

This chapter is, in short, about how the best stories can be co-opted by their audience, and how that co-optation is almost always reactionary, meant to preserve the qualities of the story that the audience loves at the expense of the challenges that the authors or even the stories themselves want to produce. How these series can respond and how they might move forward can tell us a lot about the future of the auteur in games generally.

* * *

When *Metal Gear* was first released in 1987 for the MSX2, an eight-bit home computer produced by Microsoft, it was the fruition of Hideo Kojima's strange effort to get into the business of gaming. Initially hoping to find a job in film production, Kojima came to see games as an avenue for his ambition to represent the world in art and became a game designer. This choice was not taken particularly well by his friends and mentors, and as Kojima says in an interview with Simon Parkin at the *Guardian*,[1] "When I announced my decision, all of my friends and lecturers begged me to reconsider. They thought I was crazy, to be honest. It was only my mother who told me that I could do whatever I wanted to in life. She was the only one."

This is the kind of heartwarming story that becomes public knowledge well after someone has become a myth, an anecdote that helps explain the quirky, idiosyncratic tendencies of an individual along his or her unorthodox path to a career. And as touching as Kojima's mother's support is, I'm more interested in the way that he describes his animating aesthetic desire as he pursued film and storytelling generally. Parkin helps him unpack this after Kojima relates that he always is making up stories and always has been, that he cannot even trust himself to drive safely because his mind is so quick to wander. "Even now, while we are talking, I find my mind wandering if I'm not careful," he tells Parkin, explaining that he has been thinking about a coffee cup in the middle of the table between them.

"OK. What's the story of the coffee cup?" Parkin asks.

"I am imagining a story in which there's a massive coffee cup that we're all sitting inside now. It's not really a story, I guess, so much as a vivid picture. But this! This is how my mind works."

Again, Kojima offers a perfectly charming answer but one that speaks to a kind of evasiveness of aesthetic—he is committed to a mimetic representation of the world around him, and he uses any means necessary to get there; he is always making up stories and has a sympathy beyond normal people to imaginative action. The vision we get of Kojima here, in a 2012 interview that is, I should say, a lovely read, is one of an untouchable mind, impossible to pin down and irresistibly admirable. This is Kojima with the edges smoothed, the Kojima of whose output you can say only positive things and for whom criticism is relegated to gender critique (more on this in a bit) and games rankings. In other words, a Kojima that isn't particularly interesting to delve into.

The games themselves tell a different story, one of a creator finding his feet during an era in which an auteur director for video games was a more plausible idea. Kojima of course had a team helping him make *Metal Gear*, but the process was more streamlined and less expensive during the MSX2 and Nintendo Entertainment System days, so we can imagine a world in which his influence was in fact as oversized as we all assume it must have been.

Metal Gear is not particularly exciting to play in 2021. It is a top-down stealth game that doesn't have much of a shooting/fighting mechanic to it. Your character, under orders from Big Boss, infiltrates the base Outer Heaven to save fellow officer Gray Fox. You play as Snake, a character we see again and again in these games, though as the series progresses, the plot summaries become far more cursory than the game plot itself, and Snake quickly becomes a metonymy for *Metal Gear* as a series. Still, at this point, he is a green soldier parachuted into an enemy base and told to focus on staying undetected as this is "a sneaking mission."

This element, so entirely crucial to every iteration of the series after this first installment, came about due to hardware limitations. As Kojima tells *Retro Gamer*: "You could not have more than four bullets with MSX, and that meant you could only have two to three enemies. You cannot make a combat game with that. So I came up with a game like [the 1963 film] *The Great Escape* where the prisoner had to escape. It was an idea born from adverse situations."[2]

In other words, Kojima's stealth ethos that animated the entirety of the series was born from a technical limitation, something that modernist poets might cheer as an example of a restriction producing interesting forms due to the nature of the constraint. Unfortunately for this analysis, the interesting elements of the game begin and end there; although the metal gear itself—a mechanical walker able to launch nuclear missiles from anywhere on earth—looks cool, the game feels sterile outside of the sneaking elements. Snake finds card keys, avoids situations, and messes around with items here and there to avoid death. In the end, he is betrayed by Big Boss, who reveals himself to be the leader of the militarist coup in Outer Heaven. Snake defeats him and escapes to fight another day.

For the first twist in a series full of twists, this one is, I admit, underwhelming. But to Kojima's credit, builds upon the plot of *Metal Gear* for the sequel to the game, also released on Sony MSX2, but not on the much less technologically powerful Nintendo Entertainment System, or NES. *Metal Gear 2: Solid Snake* picks up where the first game left off, sending Snake to a military compound run by Big Boss, who survived the ordeal in Outer Heaven and now runs a paramilitary base full of African child soldiers and mercenaries. The politics of *Metal Gear 2* are a bit denser than those of the first game and touch on the imperialism, but the game's politics are not so complex that we need to dwell on them here. Instead, it's worth looking at the way Kojima treats his real ideological hobbyhorses: the soldier and the nuclear weapon.

In *Metal Gear 2*, we see Gray Fox return, this time as a loyal soldier for Big Boss, and we see more characterization all around. The return of Big Boss speaks to the already circuitous paths these games will take to use life, death, and the promise of continuity to produce their sequels, and *Metal Gear 2* is the first time we see how complex the plotlines of this series will become. Big Boss is insistent that you, Snake, join him in this, a soldier's paradise. For the first time in the *Metal Gear* games, we are given the philosophical perspective that soldiers, after they see war, can never return to society, that instead it is best for them to secede to their own society built upon conflict and violence, a paradise of combat. The concept is more grandiose than convincing, to be fair, but the concept of the soldier as somehow less human or differently human is a theme throughout all of the *Metal Gear* games from this point on, and the penultimate battle in the game—a fistfight to the death with Gray Fox while surrounded by land mines—speaks to the death-wish machismo inherent to this kind of expression of desire. The homosocial elements of *Metal Gear* also introduce Kojima's strange gender issues in this game, as the female love interest—a reporter-cum-soldier—is ghosted by Snake at the end of the game as he flees her request for a date by disappearing into the wilderness of central Africa. Women in *Metal Gear* are typically trivialities or meant to embody tragedy, while men represent the tragic totality of violent ambition.

In a more salutary set of interests, Kojima also extends his concern over technology and the nuclear bomb, as metal gear returns, in a reveal as dramatic as Big Boss's own revelation that Snake is his son, though the scientific elements of that revelation are made clearer in the next two games. But the scientific web of destruction that relies on the threat of nuclear weapon develops further in *Solid Snake* than in its predecessor, not least of all due to the underlined threat of metal gear as a sort of walking, borderless nuclear arsenal. The machine itself embodies the fear of destabilization that Kojima speaks to as much as Big Boss's strange mercenary nation-state and does so more effectively as a much more plausible sort of specter of science gone awry. Furthermore, the game plays with the intersections between technology and espionage on a much more granular scale. The father of Snake's love interest, a well-known nuclear scientist, has been kidnapped by Big Boss to implement metal gear. The only way to help him is to read the original guide that came with your game, perform some code breaking, and free him from a sweltering prison cell. Then you discover that this doctor has killed the scientist you initially came to rescue, torturing him in the interest of using his intellect to aid Big Boss and the path of destruction. For Kojima, intellectual corruption corrupts absolutely.

Though these first two games feel primitive by contemporary standards, there's a sense of the future, particularly in *Metal Gear 2*, and that sense of scientific paranoia, global war, and the totality of a soldier all crystallize in the next game in the series, *Metal Gear Solid*.

* * *

Released for Playstation in 1998, *Metal Gear Solid* is another game that is tricky to historicize due to years and years of hype, plaudits, canonization, and personal weight. It was one of the first games that a lot of people saw played on a thirty-two-bit system, and for many it heralded the next generation of games that came to define their childhood and young adulthood. Referring to retrospective reviews likely offers little more than rose-colored lenses. That said, the reviews of the time were primarily either positive or, interestingly, confused. Jeff Gerstmann, of *Giant Bomb* fame, wrote on *GameSpot* that *Metal Gear Solid* "stands as more of a work of art than as an actual game" and warned players that "once you know exactly what to do and skip as much plot as possible, you can run through the game in three hours or less."[3]

Gerstmann's critique of the game isn't incredibly popular now, and if it was, it would be for reasons he himself probably wouldn't appreciate. As a game that appears on many top-ten games lists, *Metal Gear Solid* has a reputation that's no less than sterling. But that doesn't mean that Gerstmann was wrong. On the contrary, he makes a fair point here—like *Snatcher* and *Policenauts* before it, *Metal Gear Solid* plays like a visual novel with stealth sections and gunplay peppered in for effect. The set pieces in which you get to fight—particularly the Sniper Wolf and Psycho Mantis boss fights—are quite fun on their own, but they're also a bit clunky and have aged poorly. The last boss fight takes place in a mine cart and feels like the kind of level that a current indie game designer would add at the last moment to make sure potential customers knew it was an action game. And this would all matter a lot more if the game were not, as Gerstmann himself says, a remarkable piece of narrative work.

The story of *Metal Gear Solid* may, I fear, sound familiar to you if you've read this far. Solid Snake, our protagonist from the previous two games, has been called in to perform a rescue mission and diffuse a splinter cell that has taken the nation hostage by hijacking a nuclear silo in Alaska and threatening nuclear war if its demands are not met. You're to rescue the DARPA Chief, who has the nuclear codes, and neutralize the terrorists. Oh, and as it transpires, metal gear is there, too, which is definitely a big surprise. Beyond this, the game opens into a vista of twists and turns, with the return of a character from *Metal Gear 2* who turns out to be your main antagonist, Liquid Snake, in disguise; to a revelation of child clone soldiers, of which you are one, as is your father Big Boss and your brother Liquid Snake; to the final revelation that Liquid Snake intends to set off the nukes to re-create Outer Heaven and build a world where soldiers can thrive.

In between all of this, there is—of course—a girl who acts in part like a love interest for Snake and in part a challenger to his abilities as a spy. But in the end, Meryl, the Colonel's daughter, is another person Snake must save, along with the bumbling Hal Emmerich, or Otacon, one of the people who helped design metal gear. If that isn't enough, there is a colorful cast of enemies and allies, including a sultry Russian woman versed in the entire history of nuclear proliferation and a Chinese naval officer who saves your progress and shares koans to boot. Indeed, with all of its abilities, this game shines most when you are in the "codec" screen, calling your comrades to get their advice on situations or simply picking their brains about their individual specialties.

This is what I mean when I say that the game feels best when it is comfortable in its shoes as a visual novel. There is nothing wrong with sitting back and enjoying the dialogue, the harsh condemnations of Russian and American nuclear weapon failures, the dangers of nuclear war, and, of course, the existential quality of war. There is even a sweet, if abortive, love story between Otacon and the enemy sniper Sniper Wolf, who you, of course, kill. Don't worry, Otacon presumably gets over it.

This dynamic of action-packed sneaking and shooting and in-depth, carefully written narrative, however, creates the first fissures in *Metal Gear Solid*, though the fissure is quite productive at this point in the series. This is because while the game itself plays like a traditional action game, albeit stealthier, the storyline plumbs the implications of *Metal Gear 2*, even reintroducing Gray Fox as a cybernetic ninja who begs Snake to repeat their deadly battle in Zanzibarland in *Metal Gear 2*. He pleads for Snake to "hurt me more!" in an attempt to regain the purity of feeling from their final battle. The motivations of many other characters mirror this desire for a return to a past they venerate. Grey Wolf is looking to relive his past, to solidify his sense of being a warrior. Liquid Snake wants to prove that he is the superior clone to his brother, attempting to secure superiority through dominance. Otacon wants to escape the implications of his scientific work in the fantasy of being a purely good person. Even Meryl wants to establish herself as her own person through battle, apart from her father, who misrepresents the mission in order to appear the dutiful military man while trying desperately to be a good father.

Only Snake seems to know who he is. Snake, who rejects those who label him as a hero not because he is humble but instead because he rejects the concept of heroes. The world is full of danger, terror, and looming nuclear destruction, and to Snake, the idea of a hero in such a world makes no sense. Not least of all due to the fact that all of the actions in *Metal Gear Solid* are taken by mercenaries or soldiers who are being manipulated and used as tools to further inflame global conflict. After fighting Snake, Gray Fox says, "We're not tools of the government or anyone else! Fighting was the only thing . . . the only thing I was good at, but . . . at least I always fought for what I believed in." Snake expresses the same sentiment more generally when he explains that "there's no winning or losing for a mercenary."

For Kojima's America, there is simply a series of battles that eventually boil down to people acting in self-interest. The only way to be a hero is to extricate yourself, live alone, and accept that you are perfectly ordinary. Each time he is called upon to be exceptional, Snake dismisses the concept, explaining that he is good at killing but that he is also an empty shell as a result. He does the right thing but refuses to take the hero's share of glory or success. Instead, he insists on disappearing at the end of the game, a departure that rings more truthfully than his quick escape in *Metal Gear 2*. Classified as "killed in action" and marked to die by a virus that kills only the clone soldiers like himself and his brother, Snake is free to live out the indeterminate rest of his life as he wants to: alone. The moral at the end of the story is that none of the game should have happened.

And so when we meet Snake again at the beginning of *Metal Gear Solid 2: Sons of Liberty*—the long-awaited sequel to *Metal*

Gear Solid—that came out on the *next* generation of gaming consoles, Playstation 2, it shouldn't be surprising that he reconnects with Otacon to run a strange little NGO/environmental terrorism concern that destroys metal gear units around the world. What was surprising was that Snake's mission of peace is seemingly stopped short during the first hour or so of the game, when the ship he has infiltrated to destroy an aquatic metal gear called Metal Gear Ray is destroyed, creating a massive environmental disaster in Manhattan Bay. Snake spots Revolver Ocelot, a villain from the previous game, in the belly of the ship. Ocelot seems to be working with Russians to sink the ship, but the rest of the world is unaware of this, and Snake, presumed dead, is branded a terrorist responsible for the catastrophe.

Flash-forward to your new protagonist, Raiden. A more lithe, androgynous protagonist, Raiden has a steady girlfriend who is, coincidentally, his contact who saves his game and gives him intel over the codec. Furthermore, our friend from *Metal Gear Solid*, the Colonel, is back. Raiden is infiltrating the Big Shell to stop a group called Dead Cell from, yes, launching nuclear weapons with the power of Metal Gear Ray. The Big Shell is the environmental cleanup facility that stands in place of the tanker Snake "sank" in the prologue to the game. Dead Cell is holding the president hostage, asks for unrealistic demands, and seems entirely unhinged, so Raiden, as the newest member of Fox-Hound, the old unit of Big Boss, Solid, and Liquid Snake, has to stop them.

If this sounds extremely similar to *Metal Gear Solid*, then you are following along. Raiden, midway through his mission, meets a man named Iroquois Plissken, who coincidentally looks and sounds the same as Solid Snake. The Colonel warns Raiden not to trust him and reminds him that Snake is a terrorist, on the off chance he should meet him, and this dynamic of distrust flows through the entire game. And the game certainly has a *lot* of plot to follow—it retains the visual novel feel of the first game with far better combat and immersive stealth sections. The number of twists and turns will give you vertigo, and if you want to hear someone talk about that plot more fluently than I, I cannot recommend Felix Biederman of the *Chapo Trap House* podcast highly enough. He spoke with me about the end of the game and its birth metaphors, prescient concerns about the internet, and existential crises on my podcast, *No Cartridge*. I won't attempt to one-up him here.

Instead, I will jump to the end of the game, where the frame of the game is revealed to Raiden and he finds out that the Colonel and Rose are made of a rapidly deteriorating AI. In fact, the entire Dead Cell situation has been orchestrated by a high-ranking group of mysterious elite individuals called the Patriots in an effort to make a new Solid Snake. Following *this* revelation, Raiden is told that he is one of the war children from Zanzibarland, raised to be a killer and then let loose in America without his memory by the first, imperfect clone of Big Boss, Solidus Snake.

Raiden is spat into Manhattan proper and told by another AI that it means to protect mankind against the evils of the internet and to force its conception of truth and objectivity into the reality of the present, thereby initiating its desired future. Raiden is asked to help it, or it will kill the real Rose, and so he does. He kills the first Solidus Snake, as the AI requests, atop the New York Judiciary Building, as Solidus pleads for him to recognize that the years he fought in the Civil War were "as real as they come, split between life and death. You ran from it! And now you've been led back to war by something less than real." Yet, at the end of the game, Solid Snake reappears—he was Iroquois after all—and Raiden, now Jack, is led into a cliff-hanger opportunity to end war entirely.

If you're confused, don't worry—I am too. But the takeaway from the mind-bending ending of *Metal Gear Solid 2* isn't the existence of a new Snake clone or the Michael Bay–inspired grandeur of a final duel on top of a historic building. Rather, it is this idea that a sequel to a game is—in the reality of the world it exists in—literally a sequel to the original scenario, an attempt to re-create the protagonist by reproducing the events of *Metal Gear Solid*. In this moment, there is a clear argument that Kojima is doing uniquely good work as an auteur—the lesson of *Metal Gear Solid* is that none of that game ought to have occurred; the lesson of *Metal Gear Solid 2* is that any attempt to re-create the spirit of those events are doomed to end in tragedy because the repetition of a scenario will never create a better or more useful hero.

Indeed, even at the end of the game, in which Snake and Raiden are given information about who the Patriots are, there is no real sense that there will be any changes if the same infiltrations are repeated again and again. Kojima seems to be leveling a critique at his own series, noting that despite the thematic changes he can make in the games, there will never really be anything new in this genre. At best it is a repetition that hopes for new outcomes while producing less and less satisfactory heroes. Snake, the game seems to suggest, is gone. And Raiden is now, too. Whomever you get next will no longer fulfill you anymore. Fulfillment doesn't come from a gun, from war, or from others, but from a critical and difficult acceptance of the material world around you, ugly as it may be. A remarkable way for the series to potentially end.

But then, the series suddenly changed.

* * *

In *Metal Gear Solid 3: Snake Eater*, we suddenly return to the past. We are still ostensibly playing as Snake, though we quickly realize that this is a flashback to the history of the clone soldiers, to the original Solid Snake, aka the soldier who became *Metal Gear*'s Big Boss. In the game, fully set in the distant past relative to *Metal Gear Solid 2*, Snake is sent to the USSR with his own commander, a woman ominously called the Boss, who defects and joins the cruel General Volgin. He must extract the Boss and destroy the

Shagohod, a proto–metal gear. When Snake finally defeats the Boss, he is told that she was a double agent by order of the United States. She had to die to give plausible deniability to U.S. involvement with the Shagohod incident. Snake is promoted to Big Boss and the game ends with a funeral for the Boss, his mentor and mother figure.

Pair this with the extremely antiwar enemies, the Fury (who channels the anger of war), the Pain (who controls stinging hornets, which reflect the pain of war), the End (an elderly, near-dead sniper who emblematizes death), and the Boss, who is the Joy (an ironic moniker since she lost her partner, the Sorrow, during World War II), and *Metal Gear Solid 3* certainly seems to be repeating the antiwar, antiheroic sentiments of its predecessors. But then, with *Metal Gear Solid 4: Guns of the Patriots*, we are back with an elderly Solid Snake and Otacon in a world dominated by mercenaries. And then we move to *Metal Gear Solid 5*, in which we get the backstory on the generation between the Boss and Solid Snake. And don't forget *Peacewalker*, the portable sequel to *Metal Gear Solid 3*, that follows Big Boss through the Cold War or *Ground Zeroes*, which provides even more context to Snake. In fact, all of the games save one—*Metal Gear Revengeance*, an action game set in the future in which your protagonist is a cybernetic Raiden who kills everyone and everything around him—follow the story of Snake. The same Snake who is no hero, who is meant to be replaceable, unimportant in a philosophical and narrative sense, who is *literally* replaced in *Metal Gear Solid 2*, much to the distress of fans, simply to prove a point. To prove a point that Snake made in *Metal Gear Solid*—that there is no winning or losing for a mercenary, there is only the next job or the next conflict. The present continues on without us, the end of *Metal Gear Solid 2* tells us, and we must get used to that.

Well, unless nothing makes us.

After fan outcry over Raiden's sudden appearance as the protagonist of *Metal Gear Solid 2*, Konami and Kojima both seem to have
acquiesced to the game's fanbase. As an article on *Industry Gamers*
suggests, Kojima's "surprise change in protagonists angered many
fans, who accused Kojima of pulling a dishonest bait-and-switch.
The twisting nature of the game's story and the sudden change in
playable characters caused a noticeable backlash against the game,
despite positive initial reviews." It goes on to say that the series
suffered serious sales losses despite Kojima's decision to shift back
to a Snake-like character and mock the Raiden character ruthlessly
in *Metal Gear Solid 3*.[4]

Perhaps this is just a recalibration by Kojima, who said in 2006
that "Solid Snake is still the main character in *Metal Gear Solid 2*"
and that Raiden is more of a Doctor Watson to Snake's Sherlock
Holmes.[5] But this cheapens the quality of the narrative, and I just
can't make that kind of explanation work. The replacement of a
hero after the discussion about the replaceability of heroes at the
end of *Metal Gear Solid* foreshadows the replacement of the hero,
which positions Raiden as this replacement even before we get to
the Solid Snake Simulation revealed at the end of the game. Why
create a plotline in which the entire game is revealed to be a simulation of the previous game, an unsatisfying replication with terrible
consequences for everyone involved, if that did not pay off with the
passing of the torch? Why leave the loaded gun on the table if the
characters aren't meant to use it?

Perhaps this is what I am missing—perhaps that loaded gun isn't
what Kojima wanted for the series, which by all accounts had become his. Perhaps the auteur with a reputation as a demanding
boss—who ensured ice cubes melted accurately in the PS2 engine
for *Metal Gear Solid 2*, only to have the technology basically unseen—is the "real" Kojima, not the narratively careful one. But I
think this may be overly simplistic. I think both Kojimas exist—the
one who is concerned with these challenging narratives and the one

who cannot get beyond the gimmicks that draw praise from the fanbase. Much like Solid Snake, Kojima takes on the role of a monolithic hero instead of an individual trying, and often failing, to produce something important.

If this seems unfair to Kojima, who does not control how the media writes about him, I have to agree. But there is something undeniably jarring about the trajectory after *Metal Gear Solid 2*, to the point that the series feels almost hijacked, changed from what it was meant to express. The themes remain in the later games: criticism of militarism, of nuclear proliferation, of mercenary states. Although the games are fun to play—and in fact *Metal Gear Solid 5* is the most fun in the series—there is something thematically less honest about these games, or perhaps more audience centered than in the first four installments. Kojima's treatment of women, purely as sexual objects and often bearing the brunt of male violence, reflects this quality of player expectation driving plot. When asked why he had included a female sidekick wearing skimpy clothing in *Metal Gear Solid 5*, Kojima responded that "once you recognize the secret reason for her exposure, you will feel ashamed of your words & deeds."[6]

The reason? She could only breathe through her skin. Is this the most outlandish plot twist in *Metal Gear* as a series? Probably not, the games absolutely embrace silly pseudo-science and always have, which frankly adds to the series in my estimation. But the concept that this is some sort of narrative choice that needed to be respected or that, in retrospect, would be understood as sensitive, is very strange coming from the person who directed *Metal Gear Solid 2*. Quiet's exposure is nothing but a choice that is meant to produce a sexy sidekick. Pairing this eroticism with a violent past as a way of justifying it cheapens not only the character, but the relationship between Kojima and the player. Certainly, this isn't the first time Kojima has used a woman as a prop in his games—Otacon's sister Emma, introduced and killed for unearned emotional resonance in *Metal Gear Solid 2*, is perhaps the clumsiest and most poorly executed character in the game.

But the pretension that Quiet's story would silence her critics when there was no real story at all speaks to the way that Kojima saw his role as an auteur: his choices didn't need narrative or thematic reasons. Likewise, the unsatisfying way *Metal Gear Solid 3* replaced Raiden with Big Boss did not require any reason or explanation from its audience other than it was what Kojima had decided for the series.

This relationship between the auteur and fans becomes a sort of self-propagating feedback loop: the auteur can do no wrong by the fans, and the fans are the ultimate arbiter of the auteur's work. Far away from the risk of adding Raiden, the later *Metal Gear* games gave the fans exactly what they wanted: a hero in Big Boss and his progeny, a lineage of war that produced exceptional men: the very thing Snake and Kojima both warned against in *Metal Gear Solid*.

But Konami has moved on from Kojima and from *Metal Gear*—the former video game giant seems content to produce pachinko machines, and Kojima has taken the next step in auteurism and founded his own Kojima Productions studio. It recently released its first game, which grapples with some of the same issues as *Metal Gear*, though with a radically different structure and narrative. In this way, Kojima shows us something we haven't seen in this book so far: What happens when creators restart a relationship with their audience after being tied to a reputation-defining project for so long? Does *Death Stranding* produce the challenging narratives of the early *Metal Gear* games or does it commit the same mistakes as the last few? The answer is somewhere in between, but the journey there is fascinating enough to warrant discussion.

* * *

Around the time that *Death Stranding* was released, I was asked to write a review of the game for *Electronic Gaming Monthly*. I revisit that review here within a framework that was not possible at the time that I originally played this game more than a year ago.

I was asked to tell readers if they would like the game, naturally, but I'm still not sure that anyone can tell you if you'd enjoy *Death Stranding*. Or, rather, if you *should* like *Death Stranding* in any objective way. The game is so powerfully idiosyncratic in its gameplay loop that you'd have to try it, for a few hours at least, to decide whether the game is any fun for you. It's a matter of taste. People are going to have dramatically different opinions about how fun this game is, and they will have a hard time pinning down why they feel that way. Imagine it this way: if I say that a sunset is beautiful, and you fire back that the sunset is garbage, there's not much either of us can do to argue the other around to our position. I think the sunset's pretty; you think it's ugly. The very idea of some sort of objective "resolution" to our argument seems silly, even if it's what we wanted.

Because I wanted to make an argument about this game that extended beyond a simple observation, I didn't spend a lot of time determining if the game looked great or was "fun." Similarly, in this chapter, I didn't spend a lot of time explaining that *Metal Gear Revengeance* is one of the most purely fun entries in the *Metal Gear* series, or that *Metal Gear Solid 5* is absolutely gorgeous and engrossing, or that *Metal Gear Solid 3* is one of the most gripping games I've ever played. Although I enjoyed playing *Death Stranding* and found it beautiful in its way, I also was struck by the fact that the only thing I could make a clear argument about was its story. Specifically, I could argue a very particular claim that *Death Stranding* makes about America, American exceptionalism, and connectivity, and how that claim, much as the claims of antiheroism in *Metal Gear Solid 3*, falls short.

Death Stranding tries to argue that America represents an insufficient and even dangerous political project, but instead of making that claim explicitly or through the narrative, the game ultimately produces a muddied, incoherent series of ideas instead of an argument. The early game presents an America that's mostly artifice—an Oval Office that's depicted through a hologram projection over a gray hospital room; devices for "linking citizens" that look more like handcuffs; and a de facto leader, Die-Hardman, wears a mask throughout 95 percent of the game. The game seemed poised to present a narrative that would attack fantasies of "going back" to the "old" days, fantasies in no short supply in our own American moment. Extra points can be given for the darkly prescient inclusion of a virus of sorts that keeps people quarantined in *Death Stranding*, a troubling reminder of COVID-19.

But as the game introduces more to the world and its narrative, this simple critique becomes muddied in a way that doesn't make it more complex but instead smooths out any contradiction or critique in favor of a happy ending in which the nation could be saved and humanity might survive another day. In other words, *Death Stranding* starts out with a pointed approach but settles on a description of America as a land of contrast, one that is not only depoliticized but politically frustrating on its own merits. To see how, though, we have to dig into the plot.

Death Stranding opens in an unfamiliar world without a lot of explanation. Through context clues and explication, we learn that the world is populated by ghosts—BTs—who can both kill and claim the corpses of humans, causing a "voidout," or a dead-body-driven bomb blast. These blasts have a staggering impact, some taking out entire cities, so bodies must be incinerated. People live underground, either crowded together in cities or on the periphery as "preppers"—a parallel to the strange bunker mentality of our own prepper community in 2021. Add to this a frequent type of rain, timefall, that ages anything it touches instantly, and roving bands of marauders who will rob you blind while knocking you senseless, and this world is a terrifying prospect. It's no wonder then that we need our hero, Sam Bridges, portrayed by Norman Reedus (an uncanny addition to the genre thanks to advanced motion capture, which reduces the more ambiguous qualities of representation into a far more determined and anodyne form). Sam steps in as an unwilling and unlikely deliverer of mankind, a savior, a force for hope during our world's most hopeless moment, doing a job that would make the bravest among us weep: that's right, he is a mailman.

Like the mailmen of our own time, he is appreciated for the hard work he does. His transformation into messianic hero comes only when he's tasked by his mother, the President of the United Cities of America, with connecting the "chiral network" across the country. Sam, who also happens to be estranged from his mother, is wary of fulfilling her dying wish but agrees when he discovers that his foster sister, Amelie, is in trouble on the West Coast. His devotion to Amelie overcomes his sincere distrust of his mother, and we begin the long and winding journey of Death Stranding. The chiral network is a sort of hyper-internet, capable of not only connecting people with information but also cross-dimensionally dilating time, which allows for the rapid construction of bridges, roads, towers, generators, vehicles, and more.

This is how the infrastructure-building element of *Death Stranding* is introduced and also how Sam's deliveries progress from a brutal slog to relative ease with the introduction of quick fast-travel and dangerous weapons. With the expanse of the chiral network serving as the game's central motivation, Kojima seems to be presenting a simple but legible parable of connectivity—Sam must unite the world, and in so doing, get over his aversion to people. This transformation is as literal as it is figurative for Sam, whose DOOMs—a strange, never fully explained disease from which much of this postapocalyptic community suffers—gives him a deeper connection to the BTs around him and who also suffers from aphenphosmphobia.

From there, the plot complicates and deepens this parable, as good plot tends to do; unfortunately for us, there are far too many obstacles. We are introduced to issues of gender, family, death, parenthood, country, belonging, paranoia, metaphysics, and more in a game that at times feels as if it's rushing through its plot in order to get back to its deliveries. As a result, what begins as a focused consideration of nation-as-family becomes a sprawling and unsatisfyingly cursory account of anything and everything that makes people human.

Kojima returns to his first love of straightforward narrative exposition, as interviews, emails, and plot options, which you need to seek out by finishing esoteric missions like pizza delivery, produce the lore of the game and the deeper story undergirding it. The issue, however, is that all of these explanatory efforts, on-screen and off, seem to focus on clarifying how the world of Death Stranding *works* practically and theoretically. Though such an explanation is of course important to any player who has trudged up and down mountains to deliver oxytocin to a reclusive prepper, the game itself has explicitly higher ambitions: it wants to make a political argument as well. It's just that the game, or Kojima, or some combination of both, never actually decides what this argument is. Or, rather, the argument is never explicitly made, apart from the way the world works—we have the Quiet problem all over again, an explanation of plotted idiosyncrasies that boils down to "well, I think it works."

Take my hypothetical from before, where we argue about sunsets. If we limited that argument to the ecological impact of brighter and more colorful sunsets caused in part by air pollution, that argument might proceed smoothly. The second one of us gets off track, though—say, by arguing that politicians and not the sunsets are to blame for ecological strife—we start getting confused. Imagine I do this again and again and again—now it's the politicians, now a secret cabal of elites, now the universities, now aliens. With each shift in the argument, the point I was trying to make becomes more distant, more generalized. By the end of the argument, we may be arguing about nothing more than taste itself again: whether we like the sunsets and eventually agreeing that we clearly disagree. This is what *Death Stranding* does.

It's a shame because the game has a fun narrative at times. Kojima's issues with women are on display but muted (outside of the strange character of Mama). He's willing to call the atrocities committed in the game "atrocities" and even pokes holes in his idealized America-via-connection through the black ops wet works that cause the protagonists and the world at large unimaginable pain. Of course, there are still terrible moments when the game is blindingly tone deaf[7]—the black director of your delivery company/country, Bridges, says that the white female president is the only hope of bringing about "Reconstructionism" in the United Cities of America. Even poor students of post–Civil War America can see the issue there. But there's something to the narrative that compels a player who is looking for a nuanced argument.

But all of this is undone by the procedural Americanness of the game. Characters exist in relation to the United Cities of America and Bridges Delivery Services, from Die-Hardman's deep commitment to the UCA project to Deadman's paranoid rule-following ("These atrocities are terrible," Deadman tells you just after revealing some dirty secrets and just before explaining he can't possibly disobey the President). There are preppers who tell you they'll never join the UCA but who will sign up on the chiral network, and others that jump right into the union, citing a need for connection and belonging. The villains in the story are nihilists, bent on extinction, which puts your goal in a strong inverted light—you're meant to connect and revive the world, bring it back from the brink.

At times, your character, Sam Bridges, seems to be on board with this project. In one of the game's final moments, he delivers one of the least enjoyable prewar speeches I've ever heard, but it's one that is deliberately committed to connection, America, and the dream of democratic individualism. Then, shortly afterward and with no clear reason why, he rejects all of those ideas and insists on going his own way. When Sam, during a corpse disposal delivery, first meets the "Bridge Baby" BB-28, who helps him see BTs, he says the babies are creepy and seems honestly repulsed by them. And then, without any real character changes other than a connection that is portrayed more as shocking physically than emotionally, Sam is so attached to BB that he refuses to "decommission" it and gives it the name of his stillborn child, Lou. Don't get me wrong, I like Lou a lot. The emotional resonance of Sam's commitment is clear to any parent and probably any nonparent, too, but it feels motiveless, like a choice that needed to happen because of a script's top-down emotional direction as opposed to a reflection of the characters who occupy that script.

Indeed, the point of the game drives the narrative in this case, with characters making decisions that are necessitated by the image at the end of the game of a united America and an open frontier. This image forces progression in the narrative, and unlike *Metal Gear Solid* and *Metal Gear Solid 2*, this progression never wavers in its path forward. The end is clearly in sight from the beginning of the game.

Once this tendency toward script progression begins to steer the central theme of the game, as opposed to motivations and decisions on its periphery, the argument the game tries to make becomes not only blurred but totally indistinct. *Death Stranding* sets out as a pro-American piece from the vantage point of an idealist: this country is worth rebuilding, and so we will do that. But midway through—without giving any specific spoilers—this vision is inverted, giving us the image of a rebuilt country that is bound to repeat the mistakes of America as opposed to overcoming them. The conclusion of the game, one might hope, would either tie these concepts together or destroy one in favor of the other. One would expect to be able to say, "Here is the way *Death Stranding* thinks about America and about the national project in general." But it doesn't—the game does not have a cogent conclusion to its central question.

Of course, there is a way I'd like to see this argument resolved: I'm sympathetic to the latter, cynical vision of America, that it is a flawed project and we deserve connection without the evils of the nation-state dragging us down. And I bet others who played the game came away hoping to see an ending that expressed the opposite position. But the game itself—what we should be premising our agreement or disagreement on—is silent on the issue. Or, rather, it says a lot but without any substance. Some characters argue against the nation-state to the bitter end. Some argue for it. And Sam, our North Star and player avatar? He changes his position dramatically and without warning depending on the situation. Without a cogent through line, the game seems to dump all of the issues it's gathered into one big box marked "America is a complex thing" before concluding that each individual is right in their own individual way and that the collective can be mean, venal, and cruel but probably still should exist.

This nonargument—everyone wins and no one loses—is disappointing in large part because *Death Stranding* is mechanically such a fun game to play and so rich in potential as a result. A game premised on boredom and repetition, on the unglamorous work of delivery, on the literal weight of packages could have been a powerful vehicle for any number of claims. Instead, the game falls back on what have been fascinating themes for Kojima in the past but now feel like obvious lodestars: fathers and sons, countries and hells for soldiers alone, and the extinction of the human race. And as these filter in, the game becomes more traditional and more cluttered, losing sight of the more staid but more important themes that flatten out in its conclusion.

* * *

In the end it simply may be enough to say that auteurism in video games always tends to entropy toward a staid and boring conclusion that upsets and inspires no one alike. Certainly this can't be the case with AAA big-budget games, as the inspirational qualities of *Metal Gear Solid* and *Metal Gear Solid 2* still land despite the less compelling or plausible arguments of their successors. Certainly this kind of narrative isn't specific to a particular kind of game or a game made well or poorly. Kojima's work is almost always fun as a game, even if the plot falls apart.

When these games become cultural touchstones in the way *Metal Gear* has and when expectation carries so much weight, the only options are to trust the auteur at the helm or cross your fingers and wish for the best. I hope there's a third option here, one that trusts Kojima's intelligence as the director of four truly wonderful games in a long-running series that, even at their least inspiring, are lovely to play and critique the way that that intelligence drove his series forward.

That heroes ostensibly occupy a place of total faith, of complete trust and infallibility, may be the corollary to Snake's "no more heroes" mentality. Even when a hero fails, as evidenced by the superhero blockbusters in our theaters, the failure is necessarily edifying and important. But when Snake fails, it isn't. It's tragic, but it doesn't have to be meaningful. Similarly, when a game developer or director fails to elevate the genre, it is disappointing but not important.

Perhaps the moment *Metal Gear* sours for me is when Kojima decides that his work is necessarily important, that the *Metal Gear* series has to serve a fanbase and a community that needs a win in terms of artistic representation. At that moment, what these games argue stops being important entirely, and the discourse becomes what the games do for the medium. But like the question of Quiet, what the games *do* is tied inextricably to what the games are about, how they work, what they attempt to accomplish. Distinction can be an important issue for incipient art like games, but insisting that there is one artist, one director, one vision that can create that distinction in gaming is dangerous.

It's dangerous for players because they stop thinking about the work that they are engaging with and consuming. It's dangerous for creators who rest on their laurels after years of incredibly difficult work. It's perhaps most dangerous for those who work for an auteur like Kojima who will never receive recognition for their work, because the assumption is that Kojima himself has done it all. Whatever the specifics of this danger, we can see its effects in the *Metal Gear* series. A series that had a truly vibrant critique of militarism, individualism, and heroism, as well as a contemporary understanding of the threat of nuclear war and privatized militaries, was reduced, due to audience demand, into a shared celebration of a particular character and intellectual property in Solid Snake. I won't call these games onanistic, but I won't say you couldn't make that argument.

Perhaps as time goes by, Kojima will have the opportunity to cut any lingering ties to *Metal Gear*, to do something brand new and fresh, in the vein of *Death Stranding*, which absolutely swings for the fences and deserves credit for that. Or, more plausibly, maybe someone who worked with Kojima will respond to the way Kojima's audience responded and start a new chain of insight and argument from the threads left behind by the auteur.

5

FALLOUT AND SHIN MEGAMI TENSEI

Whose Apocalypse Is It Anyway?

How do we imagine the future after capitalism? Or, if we wanted to make it less political, how do we imagine the future as a different space than the one we are in right now? We could always turn to science fiction, the worlds of the future in gleaming white and chrome, but I think there's a real urge to turn to our favorite apocalyptic fiction and to imagine our different future in the ashes of our current one. This is no different in games, where apocalypse runs wild as a popular narrative trope, but are all apocalypses created equally? When we play the Americana-soaked apocalypse of the *Fallout* series, is it the same apocalypse as the demon-infested *Shin Megami Tensei* series? And if these apocalypses are not the same, then do both (or either) imagine a world outside of capitalism? Or do they simply reassert the old binaries of the system in new, bleaker colors? In this chapter, we tackle the end of the world and ask which apocalypse gets us closer to the world we all deserve and which games best simulate this futurity for us.

* * *

When academics gather, either in groups or alone at their Mac-Books to write articles, they're often warmed not only by a fire in the hearth or the knowledge of upcoming tenure, but also by a series of useful sayings they know they can use in a pinch. Typically, these sayings come from famous scholars in their field and succinctly express some kind of maxim that needs to be laid out before the rest of the claim can unfold in a conversation or an essay. For instance, if you were a literary critic, you might have some bookmarked passages in your library to help you explain that form and content are two sides of the same coin, or perhaps that the gaze of the reader and the intention of the author are often at odds, or even that the novel itself as a genre is a product of capitalist expansion. These chestnuts of wisdom are never enough to be the central focus of a serious scholarly claim; they're starting points for those claims—a kind of species-wide knowledge for the people who make up the intellectual class of American (and global) society.

One of the most popular of these claims, particularly in English departments, is Fredric Jameson's claim that one can more easily imagine the end of the world than imagine the end of capitalism. Or, rather, it's Jameson's paraphrasing of that claim—"someone once said," he writes in "Future City," "that it is easier to imagine the end of the world than to imagine the end of capitalism."[1] To me this attribution always called to mind the nu-metal band Powerman5000, who claim that an ominous monologue that opened their hit single came from a book that they found in a thrift store, subsequently lost, and—as far as they knew—conveniently could never be found published anywhere again. In other words, much like this long-lost book, it's likely this quote comes from Jameson himself and is attributed to someone else as a way to make it seem more anecdotal, more a part of the collective unconscious of Marxist intellectuals.

And in using this rhetorical flourish, Jameson has successfully distracted decades of readers, including yours truly, from the follow-up sentence in which Jameson *revises* his own paraphrased bit of wisdom: we can now, he says, "witness the attempt to imagine capitalism by way of imagining the end of the world." This is a tricky formulation, and one that is complicated both by Jameson's insistence on moving immediately to a general consideration of history as a concept, as well as the essay's material focus on a postgrad seminar by Rem Koolhaas. The actual promise of this sentence—that we can start to think about the reality of the capitalist system by imagining it stripped from the veneer of civil society entirely—is left as an aphorism of the sort that is too often not pursued. But for Jameson we might forgive the quick abandonment, as the idea of imagining apocalypse from his patented materialist lens is no easy feat, and his quick thought experiment of performative shopping malls where "to shop does not require you to buy" muddies the water far more than it clears it.

What Jameson might have been able to use, however, is working knowledge of apocalypse in video games. These simulations of reality have long represented economic systems of exchange apart from the world as a byproduct of imagining the end of society itself. Like a lot of science fiction or futuristic genre work, the video game genre has used the narrative liberty it is given to leap forward in time fifty to five hundred years in order to imagine some strange world that is, at its core, strangely familiar. The echoes of William Gibson's popular 1984 science fiction novel *Neuromancer* are clear in the city streets of Midgar in Square/Square Enix's *Final Fantasy VII*, and even before then, the threat of futurity was solidified by robots gone berserk in Capcom's *Mega Man* and the resurrection of Hitler's brain into a networked war machine in *Bionic Commando*. In fact, most of the chapters in this book have one or more games set in a near future that looks a lot like our world but with alarmingly fewer regulations on grift, theft, and corruption—or, in other words, alarmingly fewer regulations on capitalism.

The depiction of capitalism through apocalypse is not, however, consistently coherent. Though we can start to see the logic of exchange more clearly as more societal trappings vanish, we also can't expect every game to depict that logic the same way. And we certainly can't expect most games to focus on the economic to the exclusion of what video games most typically bring to the table. Whereas *Metal Gear Solid 4*, as we saw in the previous chapter, is focused on a future dominated by Blackwater-esque mercenary states driven by acquisition and profit, the game uses this to further its narrative about the ways that war winnows away subjectivity and replaces it with meaningless honorifics. Although a game like *Mega Man* pays lip-service to the replacement of human labor by automatons (before revolting, most of the original eight "robot masters" in the game ostensibly perform menial labor like mining or machine repair), you'd have to take the most blurred academic reading of the game possible to interpret that as anything but background noise and set dressing by a wonderful platformer. In other words, the actual content of the games themselves is not determined by the fact that the apocalyptic setting puts our own socioeconomic system into clearer focus; depicting capitalism, it turns out, isn't ipso facto criticism of capitalism.

That said, games that are strictly concerned with the end of the world are likely to be more concerned with the way the world operates after everything we know crumbles to dust. Much as Jameson's mysterious interlocutor suggests, apocalypse often leaves everything unrecognizable except for the systems by which we exchange money for goods. And if Jameson is right—and I'd argue he is—this system that's left as the sediment of society after collapse can help us understand the ways that our society operates pre-collapse. But the benefit of video games as opposed to thought experiments or extrapolations of current crisis thinking is that video games are fully wrought visions of the future and as such operate as arguments about what the future could come to look like and should come to look like.

Two series in particular have a lot to say about apocalypse, the *Fallout* series and the *Shin Megami Tensei* series. The conclusions they draw, however, are radically different.

Apocalypse is, truthfully, all these series have in common with each other; however, the nature of the worlds they depict through the course of their series produce diametrically opposed conclusions to the question of how capitalism structures a society. And in focusing—as they must within their genre—on the economic, the exchange, the acquisition of weapons and advantages, they posit a world that exists beyond our current moment in history, but that may or may not exist beyond capitalism. How the series evolve over time and what their final claims are differ greatly and present new complexities but suffice it to say that in *Fallout*, the market survives the nuclear holocaust. In *Shin Megami Tensei*, the market is already dead but doesn't know it yet. What these games say about the nature of capital and of the modern American and international state of global hegemony springs entirely from these conclusions. Without further ado, let's see how they get there.

* * *

In 1997, Interplay Productions put out a game that was destined to be the sort of cult classic that only could be pulled off in the 1990s, when access to the internet was readily available but not particularly useful in the instant-access-of-knowledge way we have now. Anecdotally, I can remember friends telling me about this game, *Fallout*, a role-playing game (RPG) in which you play a survivor in a postapocalyptic world after the nukes fell. It was supposed to be bitterly satirical and bitingly funny and completely fit the mold of the kind of game that "wasn't for kids." This was review gold for the late 1990s, when games, comics, and most nerd culture was trying to establish itself as a serious occupation for adults (who had disposable income to blow) and not just for kids (who did not). Put simply, it made for a compelling game idea that I remember more than a few friends gushing over.

On the other hand, though, *Fallout* was something of a victim of the time it was released, specifically the period before 2003, when console gaming and PC gaming were typically set apart from each other as a rule. The current ubiquity of PC and console ports of games or, even better, games simultaneously released on PC and console was not a reality in 1997, when even the most popular PC games like *Starcraft* or *Diablo II* were available only on computers. The lack of credible or popular PC versions of *Sonic the Hedgehog* and *Super Mario* should tell you how little things changed when the perspectives were swapped (though a few strange PC ports do exist, and a few freeware labors of love can be found through a quick google search, but that is another book entirely). Put simply, the cross-pollination of games between computers and consoles was not available in the market yet and would not be widespread until after Microsoft joined the console race with the Xbox in 2001.

So although *Fallout* got a lot of press and a lot of erudite support from "smart" gamers, as well as awards for RPG of the year from *GameSpot* and others, the sales of the game were good but not overwhelming. According to *PC Gamer*, the initial sales of *Fallout* totaled around 53,777 by the end of 1997, and this would balloon to 144,000 by the end of 2000, per *GameSpot*. This is nothing to sneeze at, but if we think ahead to our next chapter and consider how well *Final Fantasy VII* sold—more than two million copies were sold in two weeks, according to *Electronic Gaming Monthly*—we definitely can categorize Interplay's first foray into the wasteland of *Fallout* a modest or limited success. People enjoyed the game deeply, but perhaps more were unable or unwilling to play it.

The unwillingness may have arisen from the fact that in 1997, the Japanese style of RPG was still the prevailingly popular one: more anime-inspired design, turn-based combat, and a simplicity in its user interface captured players via, primarily, console-based games. We could say that the American RPG, or CRPG (literally computer role-playing game), followed along the *Dragon Quest* path more than the *Final Fantasy* one, focusing on story, yes, but foregrounding the complex, individuated character design and mechanics that were first seen in *Dungeons and Dragons*. This complexity helped align CRPGs with the PC or Mac, given that the number of inputs on a keyboard allowed for far greater possibility than the inputs on a controller. But surely the opposite is also true: the deeply complex control sequences in CRPGs alienated players who just wanted a story without the trouble of learning a whole system of play first.

For whatever combination of these reasons, *Fallout* was an RPG gem that didn't reach the audience we typically expect RPG gems to reach. And as a result, its legend perhaps grew even beyond its content; the game itself is, I admit, fantastic, and even now, the interface feels only slightly clunky, which is no small feat for a twenty-three-year-old game. But the humor and politics feel less fresh, and although the game has a reputation for biting satirical wit, the humor relies on a nostalgic pang for 1950s-style aesthetics and a surprising amount of hyperviolence. Indeed, the plot of the game is deceptively simple: find a water chip so that your fallout shelter/bunker survives and then, after saving your community from thirst, destroy the threat of invading Super Mutants from the wasteland. There's nothing particularly satirical or funny about this central plot, and it's not all that distinguishable from contemporary paranoia over invasion by the Other. But the plot isn't what sets *Fallout* apart.

On the contrary, what was and is so fun about *Fallout* is that you get free rein to wander the wasteland and get to know its strange and often crooked or criminal inhabitants. To that point, one of the earliest patches in *Fallout* changed the game's win condition, allowing players thirteen years of game time to finish off the Super Mutants as opposed to five hundred days, in an effort to encourage and reward exploration of the world over the completion of the plot. In the world, your character—either a premade protagonist or your own custom "vault dweller"—can speak his or her mind, make good and bad choices, steal, kill, and die. The interesting thing about *Fallout*, to be plain, is that you are put in the middle of a wasteland and then told that you are permitted to do anything there, so long as you understand that every action has both intended and unintended consequences. The asides of humor and nostalgia season this exploration impulse, but the game is chiefly about acquisition and exploration, mastery of a map and a scenario in the *Dungeons and Dragons* sense.

Mastery, of course, only occurs via barter, trade, and exchange. Bottlecaps—another nostalgic touch—are the currency in *Fallout*, but you can trade favors or tasks or the threat of violence to get what you need as well. Everything, however, has a value to it, and the vault dweller is given a need at the beginning of the game: "find a water chip, or the whole bunker dies of thirst." As such, you are begging, borrowing, and stealing (literally) in order to acquire the first goal of the game, and the market is thereby powerfully asserted by the game. The world may be over, but everyone still has to work to get by.

This situation is relatively unchanged in *Fallout 2*, 1998's sequel to the first game. As can be intuited from the proximity of the games' release dates, *Fallout 2* is almost more of a continuation than a real sequel to *Fallout*, though the scenario is new and the game does have some significant technical improvements over its predecessor. But beyond smoother, more enjoyable gameplay, the plot was largely unchanged: you, a descendent of your character in the first game, have to locate a device that can help grow food for your town in the wasteland. Along the way, you encounter more mutants, monsters, and the old members of Vault 13 and succeed in killing the bad guys, saving the good, and bringing prosperity and sustenance to your town.

So *Fallout 2*, which sold as well as *Fallout* and gave players the same sort of immersive world and simple story as *Fallout*, was effectively a sequel in the truest sense: a reiteration with a difference. *Fallout Tactics* followed in 2001 but was enjoyed more for its quality as a game rather than as a successor to the strange, persistent aura around *Fallout* and *Fallout 2*. For a while it seemed like this game would be lightning in a bottle, albeit striking twice, fated to cult status and a sizable role in the history of CRPGs if not video games in general.

And then, ten years after *Fallout 2*, Bethesda Game Studios created a sequel that would shepherd *Fallout* from a cult series to a major part of the gaming marketplace. In doing so, though, it would channel the wry humor and repetitive plotline of the first two games into a more conservative, restorative vision of humanity that would come to characterize most of the series—with one important exception.

* * *

In the 2000s, remakes and reimaginings were at the forefront of the gaming industry, as they so often are. But unlike the remakes and remasters of today, many of the games that were resurrected on Playstation 3, XBox360, and Gamecube next-generation consoles were modernizations along broader aesthetic terms. Nintendo's 2D platformer giant, the *Metroid* series, was transformed into a 3D first-person shooter with 2002's *Metroid Prime*. The next chapter discusses the way that *Final Fantasy* entered the world of massively multiplayer online (MMO) RPGs, branching into the vast reiterative content of that genre out of its more contained narrative format of the past, with 2002's *Final Fantasy XI*. And 2005's *Resident Evil 4* shifted the series from its survival horror roots toward a mix of high-speed rail-shooting mayhem and campy horror pulp. These are just three of many examples I could reference here. With the ability to do more graphically and a greater capacity for speed and world size in the new consoles, many developers were trying to situate their franchises for the future with radical changes to their thematic and aesthetic character.

Fallout was no different, though it arrived later. This was in large part due to industry politics. Interplay sold the *Fallout* license to Bethesda Studios, scrapping Black Isle Studios and the original *Fallout* team's own sequel, *Van Buren*. After the sale to Bethesda, *Fallout 3* had to wait for the completion of the equally enormous and profitable *Elder Scrolls IV: Oblivion* before development could begin in earnest. And from there, if industry interviews are anything to go on, the project needed to find its feet before it hit the ground.

The game developed largely along the same linear lines as previous *Fallout* titles, at least until the introduction of the ending. Todd Howard, who directed the game and has become almost synonymous with Bethesda Studios, revealed that the original game design had twelve endings. This seems like an appropriate amount, certainly, maybe even more than anticipated. However, *Fallout 3* was built with player agency in mind, and though previous games had produced the sort of open world for which the series had become famous, Howard's vision for *Fallout 3* eventually encompassed "over 200" discrete endings determined by player actions in game.[2] Furthermore, the game began its development in 2004, was described as "a fairly good ways away" in 2007, and finally was given a playable demo in 2008. As it grew, so did the technical intricacies, including the aforementioned endings, but also more gore, technical targeting, and in-universe gimmicks that were, I'd argue, an attempt to pay homage to the (still probably displeased)

Black Isle Studios developers. Then, finally, the game—the game that was perhaps most controversial for being a *first-person Fallout*, as opposed to an isometric third-person game—was in the wild and getting rave reviews.

I'll pause here for a moment to clarify that little aside above. First-person games are games like the *DOOM* or *Wolfenstein* franchises, which put the camera where the main character's face should be, so that you are seeing through the perspective of the main character, the "I" of the game. A third-person game is more complicated from a camera perspective and can, technically, describe any camera angle in a game where the character is represented as a full-body figure, as someone who occupies the "third-person" role in English-language conversation, the he/she/it/they role. In the case of *Fallout*, *Fallout 2*, and *Fallout Tactics*, the game was presented from an eye-in-the-sky perspective, with the map tilted at a slight backward angle, so the player sees the world as a panorama of sorts. Your view as a player is much closer than, say, the zoomed-out map from a *Civilization* game, but it's also far enough out that the game can look like a chess board if you squint, with individual characters that can be clicked on with a mouse and given commands.

This camera angle is popularly known as an "isometric" one, and it essentially follows the same logic your cool textbook doodles did in fifth grade: like a cube or a cool *S* drawn during class, the games that utilize isometric views are not 3D but trick the eye into thinking that they are. This allows for a level of depth in the field of vision that cannot be accomplished easily in first-person camera views, if only because a landscape naturally has more detail in it than a snapshot: the reason people call a generalized account of a creative process a "thirty-thousand-foot-view" isn't just because it makes the creator want to jump out of a plane, but rather because it's the intricacy without depth that distance provides. On the other hand, first-person views give a sense of immediacy that lends itself to a shooter, the close quarters and up-close perspective aligning the player with the nervous energy that makes fast-twitch action and violence so addictive.

So the announcement that *Fallout 3* switched to a first-person shooter was puzzling, much as it was for the *Metroid* franchise when it pivoted from a flat 2D straight-on camera view (otherwise known as a platformer) to a first-person shooter. But *Metroid Prime*'s success, as discussed earlier, could be seen only if you squinted. There's not a rule saying a shooter can't be fun as a platformer and as a 3D world; *Wolfenstein*'s own journey to 3D had demonstrated this. But an RPG? Specifically, a tactical RPG that relied on *Dungeons and Dragons* dice-roll mechanics and statistics and put a premium on dialogue, player choice, and world building over any combat mechanics? Could *Fallout* still be *Fallout* if it changed so much?

The answer, it turned out, was a resounding "yes." *Fallout 3* was and is a massive critical and market success and has now spawned two sequels in the same 3D world. *Morrowind*, the first-person foray into the fantasy world of the Elder Scrolls, gave Bethesda some practice in making this sort of transition work, but it was a genuine coup to extract such success from an old franchise whose cult-classic fans cannot conscience even small changes to their favorite games, let alone an entire shift in direction and content. If nothing else, people were surprised how much it felt "like a *Fallout* game."

That is, not surprisingly, ultimately the problem with the series from *Fallout 3* through *Fallout 4* and *Fallout 76*. What the first-person perspective did, essentially, was remove the player from the omniscient, almost anthropological role of observer and refigure him or her as the central point of view for the game itself. First-person not only shifts the perspective of the game functionally and formally but symbolically, as well, and the central premise of *Fallout* changed ever so slightly with that perspective. Whereas the first

games were straightforward forays into seemingly subversive humor that resolved into normative restorations of the American
dream of expansion and acquisition, the first-person sequels felt
more like Manifest Destiny–cum–superhero comic books. Everything done within the world of *Fallout 3* is done without the feeling
of frailty and danger that suffuses the first two *Fallout* games; the
protective shell of the first-person perspective normalizes the world
around the player as a reflection of his or her own point of view,
thus the strangeness of the wasteland is immediately something to
conquer as opposed to a storytelling motif.

In other words, even if you ultimately don't buy that the first
two *Fallout* games are powerfully subversive of traditional
American values, I think you have to admit that they are at their
core an exercise in role playing in the traditional sense. They force
the player to occupy the position of a character that is, as a survivor
of a nuclear holocaust, wholly unlike the player. As a result, much
of the tension in those *Fallout* games revolves around making
choices that feel only a little bit like your own: Do you shoot the
craven boss of the company town to facilitate your goal or do you
let him live? Is that your choice or your character's choice? And
what is the difference? These are worthwhile questions, and their
answers depend on the reader's experience and reaction to the
world crafted by the writers; this perhaps is ultimately why the
Black Isle *Fallout* games (*Fallout* and *Fallout 2* specifically) still
feel like winking, subversive products despite a normative storyline. They are not so much the product of their central narrative, but
of all the stories *around* the central narrative that tentpole the world
of the game.

Not so in *Fallout 3*. Much like Bethesda's later *Elder Scrolls*
games like *Oblivion* or the omnipresent *Skyrim*, the point of the
game is self-definition. Instead of asking players to position themselves as arbiters of a world they cannot understand, the first-person Bethesda titles present a world that the players can mold based

on any given playthrough's whims. And, I should admit, this makes for an enjoyable experience—you can play through any of these games reasonably sure you won't be missing anything you want to do because most quests are not mutually exclusive. You find yourself making hard choices, but ultimately the hard choices are hard because they involve choosing among different ways to actualize your agency via your character, not because of moral or ethical questions. Any question or choice posed to you in *Fallout 3*, and even more glaringly in *Fallout 4* and *Fallout 76*, is less a question of "what is the most consistent, responsible, or appropriate choice?" and instead a question of "what choice will the game most reward me for?"

As a result, despite Bethesda head Todd Howard's efforts in creating multiple endings, most people who play the Bethesda group of *Fallout* games (*3* and *4* specifically) likely do so not for the central or even the branching plots, but for a kind of immersive level-grinding, self-improvement process. In *Fallout 4*, particularly, the plot is incredibly thin and fairly schmaltzy, following your survivor as he or she attempts to avenge the death of his or her spouse and save their son, Shaun. You hear far less from defenders of *Fallout 4* about how that plot rounds out—a surprise ending that sees the son, Shaun, turning into the villainous center of the plot— and much more about the way that the game approaches base building. Indeed, *Fallout 4*'s home-building section, where you can construct a structure to protect your character against the slings and arrows of mutants and rival factions, is one of the most celebrated parts of the game, and one of the places where the fanbase's creativity shines. It is, however, mostly another way for players to feel like they are getting the most of the world they've been given, a way to further enjoy the sandbox.

This sandbox becomes more shapeless in 2018's critical and commercial flop *Fallout 76*, ostensibly a *Fallout* game that doubles as a massively multiplayer online role-playing game (or

MMORPG). Plagued with bugs, the game has been a universal flop with little fan interest, so I won't pile on here. Suffice it to say, the most radical departure you can take from the listless, self-involved kernel of *Fallout 3* is to the world of an MMO. This of course is not to denigrate the genre itself, as my own opinion of *Final Fantasy XIV* in the next chapter attests, but to say that making the self-involved world of the Bethesda *Fallouts* even more self-defined and empty of character-driven otherness is a good way to smooth the edges of any remaining narrative discomfort from the first two games.

* * *

After spending so much time arguing that the first-person perspective informed the sense of self-directed satisfaction in those games, it may seem strange that I'd now turn to a dungeon-crawling, traditional RPG game series like *Shin Megami Tensei*. Part of the distinction between the first-person perspective we see in *Fallout 3* and the one we see beginning in 1992's *Shin Megami Tensei* is generic: the dungeon-crawl first-person perspective, wherein a character advances one square per move in a sprawling map and that progress is seen from the character's eyes as opposed to an omnipresent top-down model as in *The Legend of Zelda* or *Dragon Warrior*, has more of a genealogical link with those isometric RPGs like *Fallout* or *Planescape: Torment* than the first-person shooters that inspired the spatial logic of *Fallout 3*.

Indeed, the first progenitor of the *Shin Megami Tensei* series, *Digital Devil Story: Megami Tensei* for Nintendo Entertainment System, was also presented in this first-person perspective, as were dozens of classic *Dungeons and Dragons*–style games. Whereas isometric angles attempted to replicate a sense of three dimensions within limited means, this first-person dungeon-crawl style attempted to produce a sense of atmospheric immersion within limited budgets and limited storage space. A world with a series of still images that the player cycles through while choosing movement and battle commands is always far more efficient than a fully rendered 3D world. Though backgrounds could get repetitive and dungeons themselves often required expansive graph paper analysis by the players, the size of the dungeons and areas these games provided far outstripped what would have been possible with even a primitive graphical interface.

Since the system of first-person was meant to overcome technical limitations, as opposed to producing an immersive individual player experience, the sense of constraint and discomfort in the player that we see in the first *Fallout* games is replicated in these early dungeon crawlers. You do not get to have your cake and eat it, too, often making for a less immediately enjoyable but more distinctive experience. Enjoyment, in fact, is one of the things that I think is most elusive when discussing the *Shin Megami Tensei* franchise; the games certainly are rewarding once you immerse yourself in them, but they don't let their players in very easily. Presented with very little context in *Shin Megami Tensei*, for instance, you are let loose in a hazy, ethereal maze where you are asked to name your first four characters and embark upon a journey until . . . you wake up in your bed. You have an email with an executable file attached that says it is a demon summoning program, and then you are sent out into the world to meet friends, run errands, and essentially exist in Tokyo, Japan, until (in a brief few minutes of game time) the apocalypse well and truly starts and demons begin killing or at least inconveniencing everyone you know and love.

This is, to be generous, a sort of trope in the *Shin Megami Tensei* universe. To be more blunt, it's a fairly standard template for the games, of which there are *many*. The major *Shin Megami Tensei* releases, what some people call "mainline" *Shin Megami Tensei*, all take slightly different approaches to this template, most famously in *Shin Megami Tensei: Nocturne*, the third game in the series in which the player-character is itself a half-demon, or demi-fiend. Ultimately, they all present the same scenario: the world begins normally, even prosaically, in school or amid teen dating drama, then irrevocably shifts to an apocalyptic space filled with demons and various groups of people attempting to gain control of the world around them. In the midst of this chaos, your character is forced to make decisions and align itself with a particular approach to the world around it. For the sake of space, I'll perform the critical violence of narrowing down these paths into the main three with which players are always presented: demonic, or chaotic; angelic, or lawful; and human, or neutral. In choosing these paths, you, the player, are forced to disappoint characters, even betray friends in order to get the ending you want, which can be both unpleasant and narratively immersive.

After the first blissful pre-apocalypse minutes, you're set adrift in a world of demons that somehow is well codified: there are businesses that sell weapons, potions, and so forth; there are groups of demons that align around iterations of the three main paths of *Shin Megami Tensei*; and there are conflicts for the player to solve. Early in the series, as in *Shin Megami Tensei*, these conflicts begin with your character trying to save a girlfriend or loved one: early in the first game, your mother is eaten by a demon you have to defeat after the fact, and your girlfriend dies imprisoned by demons. Familial connections do not have a long shelf life in *Shin Megami Tensei*.

Indeed, the only thing you're urged to decide throughout the life of the game is in what way you plan to survive in this fallen world you're presented with. In *Nocturne*, this becomes a balancing act between different "reasons," or philosophies, which are spread between Randian self-interest and Nietzschean will to power, as well as a sort of noble self-sacrificing destructive instinct to end the world properly instead of letting it live on in an apocalyptic state.

In the most recent mainline game, *Shin Megami Tensei IV*, you begin the game with a set party of friends and are required to betray two of them in order to save or doom the prelapsarian agrarian world where you begin and the fallen Tokyo below it, beneath the ground of the agrarian utopia. *Shin Megami Tensei: Strange Journey*, the fourth game in the series and the one just before *IV* (trust me, the numbering is even more confusing if we delve into it), is perhaps the most unique in this way, as it involves the protagonist of the game and its team trying to stop an apocalyptic event in the Antarctic. But much like the other games, your first-person view is given none of the comforts of home, and your decisions and conflicts are mediated through the lonely expanse of the arctic. Although this game is unique in the series for allowing for a "happy" ending, even this optimism requires the permanent isolation of your team and an uncanny transformation of the world as we know it. In other words, even if you get the "good" ending in a *Shin Megami Tensei* game, there is not a lot of comfort or familiarity in it.

This is what makes *Shin Megami Tensei* so effective as an apocalypse game, the fact that it is unwilling to give you a handhold of the ordinary. Even the battle system of the games, which relies on the collection and merging of demons into more and more powerful allies, is built upon complex, almost impossibly rarefied tiers of evolution, ascension, and combination such that a "complete" playthrough without a guide would be almost impossible. The demons you encounter and "align" with don't give you hints; they are demons that are just as incoherent and out of sync as the horrible world your protagonist is stuck in. There are of course touches of the familiar if you are a fan of the series, as demons and placenames recur, and the Spike Lee–esque flair of Tokyo being a main character in most of the games helps this familiarity along. But by and large, each game repeats the same trope again and again to greater effect each time: you're alone at the end of the world, and you still have to make hard choices.

The mechanic of alignment in these games as concerns player choice, particularly the micro-decisions that determine which of the three main paths your character takes in the end, has long vexed players in terms of their seemingly arbitrary and tricky management. In *Shin Megami Tensei IV*, the neutral ending is the most thematically satisfying of the three, but the management of the ending itself is beyond tricky, involving a deep mathematical calculus that is best figured out via what we in the games writing business like to call "looking it up on the internet." In *Nocturne*, the "true demon" ending is the fullest, and it requires several optional bosses, a massive optional labyrinth, and the patience of Job. Many people have said this nontraditional way of opening up endings, particularly the number of hoops you have to jump through, marks the *Shin Megami Tensei* games as particularly unique in a way that, anecdotally, I have heard people describe as very "Japanese." I'd push back against this impulse to wave away as some sort of cultural gap what Jeremy Dunham described in his review of *Nocturne* as the "bizarre" story and setting of the *Shin Megami Tensei* games.[3] In fact, I think the strangeness of the series has little to do with the way in which it is Japanese and much, much more to do with the way it is *not* American.

Individuality, heroic narratives, and the agency of the main character are the primary things that we see in the *Fallout* series that are absent in *Shin Megami Tensei*. And although the player is given a number of obvious paths in the *Fallout* games, particularly in *Fallout 3* and *Fallout 4*, the *Shin Megami Tensei* games are uninterested in providing an easy branching path; its choices lead to frustrating, depressing, or even distressing scenarios for the player. Ultimately, though, this is simply an approach to the apocalypse that eliminates the exceptionalism of *Fallout*: you may be in similar situations when you're asked to get a water chip and when you're asked to navigate a demon-infested world, but in the former you are guaranteed a path to success and redemption for the world, whereas in the latter, you simply can limit suffering. In other words, for the *Shin Megami Tensei* series, the end of the world is, in fact, the end of the world, give or take a few vestiges of doomed hope. In *Fallout*, the end of the world is an obstacle to be overcome, the beginning of something as opposed to the end. In the former, apocalypse happens to you, and in the latter, you happen in the midst of the apocalypse. These two impulses can't be held in one's hand at the same time without political dissonance and contradiction, the kind of contradiction that might clarify both approaches while asserting a third, new approach to the way the world ends. Games that take this approach must necessarily balance optimism and pessimism, the ability to change the world and to be changed by the world, and very carefully but potentially could produce a new vision of the apocalypse that could show us a new possibility for thinking about the end.

Fortunately for us, we have such a game in *Fallout: New Vegas*.

* * *

Well, we have *parts* of a game like that in *New Vegas*. The game is a fan favorite and a bona fide cult classic, and like this type of media in film and music, it represents a frenzied, idiosyncratic, unfinished shout of energy that has, as a result, some unpolished edges. In fact, we'll disregard the reviews when the game came out, if only because they were preoccupied not with the story or the narrative-aesthetic approach of the game, but with the fact that the game itself didn't work very well. Obsidian Entertainment was asked to take on this expansion/sequel of *Fallout 3* as Bethesda was—stop me if you've heard this one before—focusing a lot of its energy on producing the newest *Elder Scrolls* game, *Skyrim*. The development cycle was fairly brief, only eighteen months, and Obsidian worked to improve or at least update nearly everything about the *Fallout 3* experience, from character models, to gunplay mechanics, to the nature of the branching storyline itself. It was an undeniably ambitious approach to a sequel, especially one that didn't have a lot of support from its parent company Bethesda.

Perhaps as a result, the game shipped with several game-breaking bugs, and reviewers were torn between recommending the project for its impressive narrative and warning players against spending money for a broken product. A patch was released one week after the game's launch, which fixed many of the problems, but the reputation of *New Vegas* suffered and the game stumbled a bit out of the gate. Again, nothing surprising and in fact an impressive feat given that Obsidian tweaked an entire game engine and developed the game for multiple consoles over eighteen months. But the review space is a harsh mistress, and the story behind its reviews was far more the focus than what it was as a game for a long time. Even years after release, Obsidian executives were revealing information about the chaos of the rushed release and review cycle, even the Kafka-esque detail that its Metacritic score missed the cutoff for a bonus from Bethesda by . . . one point. A score of eighty-four cost everyone at the studio an unspecified payday.[4]

Controversies surrounding reviews, reception, and the like are one of the things that mark *New Vegas* as a cult classic. But the game also has the more crucial element of cult entertainment going for it, in that it is unironically enjoyed by a growing group of die-hard loyalists. Cult classics often get wrapped together with "ironically enjoyable" cinema or music. Ultimately, this is subjective, and one person's so-bad-it's-good is another's diamond in the rough, but it is important to note that, of the next-generation *Fallout* games, *New Vegas* is convincingly the best of the bunch.

As a result, it enjoys the continued enthusiasm of a game that didn't get its due when it was released rather than the second life of a truly bad game ("let's see how bad this really was" as was said of *Superman64* or *Sonic 06*). The game inspires retrospective looks back like one[5] from *Eurogamer*'s Emma Kent from 2019, in which

Kent praises the game's approach to resource scarcity and psychological terror a full nine years after its release. At the core of this praise is Kent's canny observation that, in *New Vegas* "even the smallest story was carefully crafted to maintain interest and deliver a rewarding kicker," lending a kind of totality to the world that speaks to the overwhelming quality of the *Shin Megami Tensei* games. The satisfaction at the end of any quest is proportional to the awe inspired by the number of directions you are permitted to go, how much you're allowed to wander through not only the original game, but its many downloadable content updates.

So let's get to that story, or to the broad outlines of it anyway, as the central narrative—a noir-inspired setup in which you are shot in the head and left for dead before searching for your killers in New Vegas—is never the focus of any memories about or current playthroughs of the game. When I spoke to *New Vegas* writer and director Josh Sawyer on my podcast *No Cartridge*, one of the questions I was asked by my audience to put to him was "what faction" he was in *New Vegas*. When he played live with me and my cohost Olivia Broussard, we were all asked the same question. When Sawyer put out his own (unofficial) mod of the game, the tweaks he made were first to gameplay mechanics and then to the game's morality system, classifying "neutral" characters as either "good" or "evil." In other words, the game's audience and, in many ways, the game itself are far more interested in asking players what choices they would make in an impossible political situation than in solving the mystery at the narrative center of the game.

Because Sawyer was not only the director of *New Vegas*, but also the scuttled *Van Buren*, our previous thinking on *Fallout* might make this point less surprising. After the narrative centrality of the first two *Fallout* games, *Van Buren* seemed to be stepping away from the centralized hero's journey that we critiqued earlier. Indeed, like the plans for the (otherwise disastrous) *Fallout 76*, the idea of *New Vegas* and *Van Buren* was cemented in the appeal of place, not story. You could explore an embodied world and decide how you fit into it, as opposed to being its savior from the word go. In this way, the promise of the game is closer to *Shin Megami Tensei* and far more pessimistic than most *Fallout* games, since saving someone you care about is almost never presented as a central concern. The crisis in *New Vegas* is deciding what kind of person you can tolerate being at the end of the world—an expansionist American spirit like the New Californian Republic? A profiteer like the gambling AI Mr. House? Or an unapologetic but Hegelian fascist like Caesar and his Legion? Or will you follow some other more marginal path and become an anarchistic individualist?

You're welcome to choose any of these options in *New Vegas*, but you can't please everyone, and you have to make hard decisions. Again, this is reminiscent of *Shin Megami Tensei*'s often-frustrating branching path: the "good ending" is very much up for debate. But due to the Obsidian team's time constraints while working on the game and the normative quality of the Bethesda vision of *Fallout*, there are clearly "evil" pathways that are so rarely taken by players that Sawyer himself has noticed. In a number of interviews, including one with me, he said one regret about the game is the fact that there is no real compelling reason to follow Caesar's Legion when playing the game. The Legion commits murder, rape, and untold atrocity even before you're properly introduced to them, and as a result, almost no one (based on current "achievement" data on Steam) follows this questline to its conclusion. This means that storylines and dialogue and content typically don't see the light of day, and more importantly from a narrative perspective, the complexity of the world begins to crumble just a bit around the edges when you consider the Legion.

But this squares with the American exceptionalism at the core of the *Fallout* franchise. *New Vegas* does its best and, in many ways, avoids the trap of exceptionalism, but because it needs to occupy the *Fallout* universe, specifically the *Fallout* universe that Bethesda has created, the world must cohere in a player-centric way. Unlike the *Shin Megami Tensei* games, you aren't given a mandate to do what you will with the world, even if that entails destroying it entirely. This freedom, ironically, gives the player far more incentive to choose sociopathic or evil paths, as the totality of the apocalypse makes choice a more arbitrary condition. You're not choosing to make or break the world around you: the world is broken and you must decide what way to change it.

Change is, in the end, the one thing missing from *New Vegas*. Caesar's Legion, ironically, represents the most likely change, but it's one that almost no one playing the game has the desire to see. The other options replicate the world around us, as opposed to some new horizon: limited resources, a series of choices that boil down to choosing individual liberties or corporate deregulation or both, and a slowly built-back nuclear wasteland. *New Vegas* gets critiqued often for not having a true "leftist" position, but I don't think of that as a flaw as much as a reflection of the realities faced by Sawyer and Obsidian. The world of *Fallout* has transformed from a "satirical" approach to the end of the world to a survival parable in which the bombs have dropped, but society—specifically American society—continues on, not exactly as usual, but not particularly far off.

This evolution isn't so far off from the first *Fallout*'s narrative message, and although I think the Black Isle *Fallout*s have a lot more to say than *Fallout 3* and *Fallout 4*, there is in all—except the beginning of your introduction to the wasteland in *Fallout*—a feeling of familiarity. This world you work your way through is blasted and mutated, but at its core, it is a recognizable Western society with all of the various power dynamics therein. Only Caesar's Legion pushes us into the uncomfortable kind of eugenic determinism that feels somehow wrong or off, but *New Vegas* is by necessity set in a world that has options that are more recognizable and therefore more appealing. This is by no means a critique of Obsidian's writing, which, it should be said, is sterling here. Sawyer's direction and vision is to be celebrated unabashedly—but the world of *Fallout* sets the limits of that vision.

In American visions of nuclear war, it seems as if the end is simply a metamorphosis into something new. It can be something worse or something comical, but it is new in a serialized way: we recognize the general outlines and are licensed to act accordingly. For *Shin Megami Tensei*, the world is over, full stop. Nuclear war often does threaten, as in *Shin Megami Tensei IV*, where the demon lord of Tokyo transmutes into a giant rock dome to save the city from nuclear devastation, thereby kicking off the main story of the game a few years before your character appears. But regardless of whether the missiles land or not, the world is infested with demons and rapidly declining. There is no returning to normal, only the quick destruction or codification of the world under a new power.

As I've said earlier, the *Shin Megami Tensei* games are often described as uniquely Japanese, a characterization that I'd caution doesn't mean all that much and tends to mystify the games in a racist and unhelpful way. But I do think the understanding of apocalypse in these games better represents a real-world apocalyptic event in no small part because modern Japan's history encompasses the real-world apocalyptic events of Hiroshima and Nagasaki in 1945. There is something far more terminal about the footage from 1945 after the real nuclear bombs fell than those re-created in *Fallout*, and that insistence on an American spark is perhaps the result of being a nation that hasn't had to live through the trauma of this kind of event yet.

* * *

Fallout and *Shin Megami Tensei* are ultimately series that are bounded by the worlds imagined in their first iterations. For *Fall-*

out, this is a twenty-three-year-long trail, beginning in 1997; for *Shin Megami Tensei*, it's since 1992. What is remarkable about these two series is how consistently they have stayed true to their visions of apocalypse, even as the games themselves morphed often in dramatic ways; the core of each series, how the games responded to the world proposed in their first iterations, remains consistent. This is frankly unique not only in this book, but perhaps in video games generally.

Even in the more far-flung examples of their main library, these two franchises are fairly staid in their approaches to their themes. *Shin Megami Tensei*'s ostensible fourth installment, after *Nocturne* and before *Shin Megami Tensei IV*, is called *Strange Journey* and takes place on an Antarctic expedition to seek out a strange power before demons invade the world. And yet, despite the world several hundred miles north operating as usual, the arctic serves as a blasted backdrop, and the world is once again in your hands as you and your colleagues can choose to use the power to destroy the world or build it again. Notably, this game allows you a sort of stasis option, something not possible in any other mainline *Shin Megami Tensei* game. But even this option ends with the world doing fine while you end up alone and isolated, a kind of martyr. Indeed, solitary confinement in the arctic still has the bleak quality unique to *Shin Megami Tensei*.

In *Fallout 76*, Bethesda's most recent foray into *Fallout*, and a critical and financial disaster, you're let loose in the wasteland outside of Washington, D.C., far earlier in the time line of the series than in any other game. Because the game was intended as an MMO experience, the world contains much wider areas, and there was a time after launch when those areas were so sparsely populated that players couldn't find a nonplayable quest character to talk to. This, of course, was a bug, not a feature, but each successive update brings *Fallout 76* closer to the vision its developers pitched, as random mobs of friends scour the wasteland, hoarding backpack nukes and building a fiefdom in a malfunctioning system. No, I will not draw the obvious parallel to contemporary American society; you can do that yourself. The upshot is that *Fallout 76*, in both its flawed release and its current role as a kind of acquisition simulator, also stays true to its roots, presenting a new world with all the same structures.

I find *Shin Megami Tensei*'s view of apocalypse more artistically generative, because it presents a narrative problem that can be challenging and even unpleasant to solve, but it teaches the player something outside his or her area of lived experience. *Fallout*, on the other hand, is a lived fantasy, a kind of power trip that echoes most of the previous RPGs that came before it, which varies the setting in an interesting way. Although it isn't as artistically productive, it is undeniably fun to experience the wasteland.

What *New Vegas* tries to do is square the fun of the *Fallout* series with the difficult thematic challenge of the *Shin Megami Tensei* series, and it runs up against the wall of series expectation. It reveals to us that *Fallout* cannot exceed the boundaries of current society. It reveals to us that, unlike the world of *Shin Megami Tensei*, the apocalypse does not reduce individualism to survival and existential panic, but rather it shifts the scene, allowing the individual to play in a new sandbox of experience. What I wonder, and what creators like Sawyer are working to engage with even now, is if the experience of empowered fantasy is central to the Western RPG genre, or if the Western CRPG can imagine otherwise and posit a different, unfamiliar world that decenters the individual in uncomfortable but productive ways.

Perhaps I'll be able to update my reading when *Shin Megami Tensei V* and whatever is next for *Fallout* and Sawyer after his *Pillars of Eternity* games are released. But for now, the politics of loneliness remain a bifurcated arena, and the mainstream American vision of the end is still optimistic, hopeful for our society. Whether this is a realistic vision of things to come, it is worth asking: In a medium in which we are given free rein to produce different worlds that exist under different and new conditions, why do we continue to reproduce the world around us?

And what will it require for us to stop?

6

FINAL FANTASY

Escape Is Other People

Our largest series I saved for last, and the question of how to manage a massive franchise like *Final Fantasy*, spanning thirty-plus years, is difficult to answer. But what we see in this chapter is that the fits and starts and wild searches to find an interpretative core that we've seen in other younger franchises are here as well. At the core of the history, the varying reception over its many years, and its balance between science and fantasy, the *Final Fantasy* series ultimately finds its feet in the company of other gamers in a massively multiplayer online (MMO) role-playing game (RPG), or MMORPG. How this paragon of capitalist gaming—subscription fees, frustrating gambling elements, and high-priced boutique items abound—was used by Square-Enix to find a salutary core is a question we can answer only by tracing the series, its pressures and expectations, and its ultimate conclusions from 1988 to the present. And the figure who is there through it all is the player, the most important character to the games themselves, the figure who immerses him- or herself in the world of the game and gives it meaning until, finally, the game gives that meaning back. Ultimately the story of *Final Fantasy* is about product interaction, but a product needs a response, a conversation with its buyer to function properly. As we see, the world of *Final Fantasy* provides a social world that both embraces its role as a commodity and rises above it in moments of camaraderie and creation.

* * *

If there is one thing that video games have aimed for consistently during their long and often fractious history, it is immersion. Immersion, that ideal state wherein your customers or players are so engrossed in your product that they feel as if it's a lived-in place as opposed to a game world, is so important because it produces a game that never has to be over. The finitude of games—as with movies, books, TV, poetry, music, and so on—is its primary commercial problem. After all, if you're running a company as a traditional capitalist might, wouldn't it be easier to make *one* game that your player base could pay for over and over again instead of many video games that they each buy once?

Within the last five years, the prevailing solution to this problem has been the concept of games-as-service. Games-as-service is a spin on the Netflix model—though you could argue that the Netflix model is a bit of a spin on games-as-service, as the concept took off with *World of Warcraft* in 2004. The game was not the *first* attempt at a subscription service nor was it the first of its genre, the MMORPG. Fantasy enthusiasts and tabletop gamers alike had been playing with possibilities online for decades at this point, from newsgroup clans to MUDs (multiple-user dungeons, which are massive text-based role-playing games). The video game version of the MMO existed, in the form of *EverQuest*, a fantasy game in a massive open world where quests were shared with other adventurers and treasure was sought through repetitive play that consumed players' lives. *EverQuest* was no small success either, spawning all the hallmarks of classic MMO reception: a truly dire reputation as an addictive game, questions as to whether it was manipulative beyond the scope of a game, massive profits, and rumors of suicides and murders driven by its power.

Never fear—those latter tragedies were not corroborated, but the fact remains that prior to *World of Warcraft*, the MMO model was a promising one. The thing *World of Warcraft* brought to the table was a worldwide appeal. There are books out there that are more dedicated to this phenomenon than mine is—Tony Palumbi's *Blood Plagues and Endless Raids*, for one—so I won't spend much time arguing for the game's mass appeal. But it's a game that at peak success boasted twelve million subscribers[1] and created, with a weird bug, a real-world epidemiological focus of study. The Corrupted Blood incident—in which a deadly (virtual) sickness with 100 percent mortality spread randomly via player contact—was a big enough deal that it has informed pandemic studies since, including the study of COVID-19.[2]

But cultural impact, as perhaps you've noticed by now, doesn't necessarily relate to popularity or commercial success. And this chapter is not about *World of Warcraft*. In fact, it's about a series that was a far more seminal inspiration for the fantasy genre in video games, perhaps more than any other, but has become something of a franchise in flux trying to rediscover its identity: *Final Fantasy*. The history of this series is probably the longest and most twisting of any in this book, and I can't say with a straight face that we cover all of it. That said, there's a fascinating through line from *Final Fantasy* to the recent *Final Fantasy XIV*, *Final Fantasy XV*, and *Final Fantasy VII Remake* that mirrors *World of Warcraft*'s journey from a stand-alone strategy game to social-subscription hub. The difference between these two franchises and why we part ways with *Warcraft* here is because long before the MMO genre and long before 1992's *Warcraft: Orcs and Humans* set the gears in motion for the franchise's ultimate success, *Final Fantasy* was grappling with the idea of how to create a repeatable genre success in the gaming world. The story of how it achieved a perfectly repeatable formula for success and why that success had to be smashed to bits to move forward can tell us a lot about the future of gaming. Indeed, what we see in this chapter is that a good model for a game that your audience loves is helpful but the ability to transcend that model and create in spite of the audience is better.

* * *

In 2021, the way we think about fantasy and role-playing games starts with video gaming, at least for the most part. Tabletop gaming, collectible card games, and all the various combinations of the two remain a vibrant and persistent scene, and it's not entirely fair to say that, for instance, *Warhammer 40K* or *Magic: The Gathering* are second fiddles to PC and console games. The swords, sorcery, and epic quests of the fantasy genre, along with the rugged individualism at the core of its narratives, fit well with a bunch of people around a table acting out their characters' actions, writing a story in real time. But still, in terms of the zeitgeist of the moment, when someone says, "role-playing fantasy game," peoples' minds drift toward video games more quickly than their more materialized gaming counterparts simply because role-playing video games have been normalized and, to be blunt, funded to such a degree that they are ubiquitous. According to Derek Strickland of gaming news site *TweakTown*, Square-Enix has reported that *Final Fantasy 7 Remake*, the newest installment in the series as of this writing, sold 3.5 million copies in its first three days.[3] And crucially, if you care about bragging rights over sales, this is with a release date directly at the epicenter of the COVID-19 pandemic. In other words, this game sold against all odds and at a truly remarkable pace. Millions of people were desperate to play this game.

This kind of culture dominance was not always the case, however. In the 1980s, while video games like *Adventure*, *Ultima*, and *Wizardry* had shown the potential for video game RPGs, the market was still dominated by Gary Gygax's *Dungeons and Dragons* (*DnD*). The tabletop juggernaut sparked a cultural phenomenon that was powerful enough to spawn both a short-lived cartoon series and a religious pamphlet by Jack Chick warning parents about *DnD*'s nascent Satanic content. In a truly bizarre 1982 article by Stuart Alsop II in the business journal *Inc.*, Gygax and his company, TSR Hobbies, are lauded as modern, quirky success stories, because this strange business of role playing as adventurers with your friends had produced three million players worldwide and millions of dollars in revenue.[4] It was with this kind of success as context that modern Japanese role-playing games began their slow rise to cultural recognition.

Although, classically, the origin of the Japanese RPG (or JRPG) style is *Dragon Quest*, released in 1986 by Enix for the Nintendo Entertainment System, I want to take a page from the history of the novel in determining what "first" means when we talk about video games. To put it more simply, saying that there is an "original" novel or video game or anything in a cultural medium is a bit of a messy claim. For instance, there are analogues between the success of PC RPGs like *Ultima* and *Wizardry* that predate both *Dragon Quest* and *Final Fantasy* and para-novelistic texts like Miguel Cervantes's *Don Quixote* or Aphra Behn's "Oroonoko" that predate the "first" novels that most of us recognize. And even those more traditional novels are up for debate as to which is "truly" first— Samuel Richardson's *Clarissa*, Henry Fielding's *Tom Jones*, and Daniel DeFoe's *Robinson Crusoe* all have a claim to the honor, but it very quickly ceases to matter which was written first. Indeed, what it comes down to for most scholars is which novel "feels" most like a novel to them: this comforting blanket of genre recognition is what people ultimately want to see in the earliest forms of their favorite art.

The same thing goes with JRPGs. Though *Dragon Quest* is as important and accomplished a series as *Final Fantasy*, the fact that

Dragon Quest features a single protagonist questing in a world of danger seems quite dated, even compared to the also dated *Final Fantasy*. The latter game maintains some modern appeal because it has a familiar format: the player guides a singular quest undertaken by a party of heroes. It is a game where you, in other words, act as both Dungeon Master and player of a *DnD* game; you as the player are able to control all of the moving parts of your party while also ceding narrative control to a story you did not create.

But much as the *Dragon Quest* games reacted to the popularity of the *Final Fantasy* structure and eventually included parties themselves, and although the competition between Enix and Square in this early arena of gaming has long been concluded in that most auspicious corporate occasion—the merger—we should not assume that the origin of the RPG video game presages a linear trajectory and evolution of the genre. Far from a hallowed and well-crafted plan of attack, *Final Fantasy*, an early response to Gygax's *Dungeons and Dragons*, wasn't born of an aesthetic passion, but from a desperation to sell the RPG genre in a video game medium. A famous urban legend says that the "final" in *Final Fantasy* comes from that fact that, as legendary series composer Nobuo Uematsu told *Wired*'s Chris Kohler, "[*Final Fantasy* director Hironobu] Sakaguchi was going to quit [if the game flopped and] . . . Square was going to go bankrupt and the designers believed that it would be the company's swan song."[5]

There's something poetic about that, but the actual significance of the story doesn't change if, in fact, we believe Sakaguchi's explanation that "to be sure, we had our backs to the wall when we were developing *Final Fantasy* . . . but really, anything that started with an *F* would have been fine for the title."[6] The point of both stories seems to be that the video game form of the RPG—as hard as it is to believe today—was not at all a sure bet, and the only way to get it to market was to sell it as creatively and aggressively as possible. This involved shifting expectations, new formal elements, and gutsy moves (not least of which involved Sakaguchi pleading with Square to produce 520,000 copies of the game to sell instead of 200,000) to make it work. But these gutsy moves were, at core, moves of industry logic, not artistic debate, and it's important to hold them in our minds as such.

But to players, the games take on the appearance of art instead of product, mostly in retrospect. The creative dynamism of industry is, to me, at least, fairly dull since it has only a single goal. There would be nothing more boring than a chapter detailing the sales figures of each game in this series, and I'll spare you that. Certainly, the numbers sold tell us something about which games are retained as models and which are discarded. Although we could tell the story of an innovator disrupting the space of a resistant industry, I think Sakaguchi and Uematsu's stories tell us something more compelling from the standpoint of their audience. *Final Fantasy*, from our perch in 2021, seems inevitable, as does its trajectory from its first installment to its fifteenth in the series. But nothing about the form or its popularity was inevitable or isolated to genius directors and visionaries; on the contrary, the games throughout the years developed through internal tweaks and challenges to the standard routine of JRPGs as well as responses to audience critique and praise.

From its beginning as an NES title, *Final Fantasy* has been preoccupied with its own identity as a series, at times precarious and at times overpowering, as well as with the idea of a player-driven narrative experience. Indeed, more than many other RPG series, *Final Fantasy* centers its players, either emptying or filling its playable protagonists to best encourage immersion into the story while also providing a sense of narrative flow outside the aegis of the player herself.

And so for most of its history, *Final Fantasy* as a series encouraged its players to occupy the role of either a blank or relatable protagonist while also asserting a disconnect between titles—the series operated primarily as an anthology series of fantastical back-drops. That is, it operated this way until recently, when remakes, next-gen road trips, and, most of all, an encompassing MMO worked to combine these plotlines and, in a move diametrically opposed to the creation of the first game in the series, center the player as not adjacent to or in control of the plot, but as literally the acting protagonist.

* * *

One of the important things I try to remember when writing or thinking about *Final Fantasy* as a series is that although the stories of the games are often gripping and compelling in the moment, they are ultimately not important from a macro view like this one. Explaining the intricacies of each game seems the thing to do when one is playing them, as the stories are all solid fantasy fare, building on their central conflicts with a litany of plot complications and obscure terms and concepts that typically shift into gameplay elements. Although this manner of storytelling is engaging in the moment that the player is deeply within the game, to summarize it is akin to the enthusiastic *Lord of the Rings* fan trying to recount the book's importance by explaining the ten-thousand-year history of elves from *The Silmarillion*: a bit much.

So, in the interest of keeping *your* interest through the fifteen flagship titles of this series, I'm going to focus on the way these games begin and set up the problems they attempt to solve over the twenty to one hundred hours following that setup. If you're a fan of this series, you may have noticed that by focusing on the flagship titles, I'm cutting out several fan favorites—*Final Fantasy Adventure*, *Final Fantasy Tactics*, *Final Fantasy X-2*, and *Final Fantasy XIII-3*. There's an argument to be made that the entire book could cover this series, since it's almost certainly the most expansive video game series popular in the United States. But that would not have painted the wide-ranging picture I set out to paint, and although every *Final Fantasy* game is different in characterization and style, they often find a clear paradigm in their plottedness. Indeed, this paradigm is what allows *Final Fantasy XIV* to remake the arc of the series some thirty years after its inception.

Rather than be held up by details and definitions of how materia is different than aether or what espers *really* are, I simplify my focus and break down the structural qualities of a *Final Fantasy* story through time. Between cultural osmosis and George Lucas, most of us have been exposed to Joseph Campbell's theories of the hero's journey—the archetypal path a hero takes across all storytelling from struggle, to doubt, to revelation. I want to complicate that standardized journey just a bit. Particularly in our contemporary moment, when we can more easily historicize and politicize the stories we've been given or we have created than the stories of hundreds or thousands of years past, we cannot give in to the temptation to replace substantive critique with quibbles over terminology, canonicity, and which protagonist we like best. To do so would flatten our analysis to a simple comparison: *Final Fantasy* seems a lot like a classic tale of heroism, full stop. What we find is that, taken as a group of individual games that vary wildly in their approach, purpose, and reception, there is nothing about this series that is remotely as simple or consistent as that thesis.

So without further ado, let's journey through time with brief pit stops at a few moments of sea change until we arrive at our ultimate destination: the current day, which I argue is the apotheosis of the series.

* * *

In the first *Final Fantasy*, we're given a fairly standard RPG plot. In fact, if we wanted to make the case that *Final Fantasy* was ripping off *Dragon Quest*, we might start here: both games begin with a hero visiting a king whose daughter has been taken; it is the player's job to rescue the princess. From there, though, *Final Fantasy* branches off dramatically: unlike *Dragon Quest*, you are not one solitary warrior on a quest, but a party of fighters, healers, and magic users. Furthermore, your party is marked by destiny—a theme we see again—by the crystals they hold. The game begins with the standard save-the-girl narrative, but the plot of the game hews closer to a typical *DnD* plot—your characters venture from town to town, solving problems and becoming increasingly more powerful while also getting closer to the "corruption" that threatens your world.

As is common with other *Final Fantasy* games, the conclusion is more complex than we need to discuss here—suffice it to say, there's time travel, shocking revelations, and a final decisive battle. The upshot of the game is that your characters travel the world and succeed, through battle, in saving it, while meeting a colorful cast of characters, as well as some series standbys like Matoya (who plays a central role in *Final Fantasy XIV*) and Cid (who, at least by name, appears in every *Final Fantasy* game). These echoes of the game obviously were not available to its audience in 1987, and what people saw in this first game was a sprawling, if not complexly characterized, adventure that involved excising all darkness from a fictional world to ultimately save it.

Final Fantasy II is where the series gets confusing in terms of continuity, at least for Western audiences. An English translation of the game was slated for release, with a prototyped release even teased by Square. The translation was difficult to pull off, however, due to the limited memory capacity of Nintendo Entertainment System.[7] And since the Super Nintendo Entertainment System that had been released as *Final Fantasy II* was nearing the end of its translation, Square punted on the translation and the subsequent game and released *Final Fantasy IV* as *Final Fantasy II* in English. Confusing? Sure, but no less so than four mismatched warriors traveling two thousand years back in time, so it didn't really affect the series' popularity.

The games existed, however, and they existed in response to the relatively massive and unexpected success of *Final Fantasy*. *Final Fantasy II* sees a group of young fighters destroyed in battle at the start of the game, and when three of the four members come to, they join a nascent rebellion against a vast empire. They discover their missing comrade in the end, who has turned and intends to destroy the rebellion, but ultimately they triumph over evil and the Empire (as well as the Emperor who has returned from hell in what can only be described as a bold narrative decision).

In *Final Fantasy III*, we see much of the same plot technique in the previous two games—a group of heroes travels from town to town, discovering problems, solving them, and getting closer to saving the world. This game, however, introduces the job mechanic to the series, in which a player can change the specific abilities of her characters in order to better tailor them to her party. This is important as the series moves forward, particularly in the technically dense *Final Fantasy V*, and reflects a turn toward even more individualized in-game modification. If the first JRPGs simply provided a "fight, magic, item, run" system of play, then *Final Fantasy III* is clearly a response to player demands for even more customization and characterization through action, a typical attraction of *DnD*. Beyond this, the game doubles down on the series' themes of light and darkness, wherein the former is the purview of the player (the title "The Warrior of Light" makes its first appearance here) and the latter the goal of the enemy.

So as we move into the next generation and new technology of the sixteen-bit *Final Fantasy* games, we can see the rapid evolution of the series shift into a fairly repeatable formula: a party of four heroes, who all represent light, often with crystals, travel together and gradually open up more space to explore as they try to save the fate of the world from a larger-than-life threat. This would serve as the basic blueprint for *Final Fantasy* games for decades to come, even arguably to this day. This framework was in response to players who wanted the emotional resonance and easy plug-and-play quality of playing a tabletop RPG like *Dungeons and Dragons* and the control of being the Dungeon Master of such a scenario. Control without interpersonal commitment and massive narrative planning drove the success of the *Final Fantasy* formula, but we see it evolve as it achieves its own hegemony beyond the tabletop craze that spawned it.

* * *

By the time *Final Fantasy IV* reached America (as *Final Fantasy II*), the series was something of a known and anticipated quantity. People looked forward to the next *Final Fantasy* game, and if you squinted, you could see how, in less than a decade, the series would be the major selling point for Sony's foray into the games marketplace. But for now, Nintendo was still *the* place for the games, and the Super Nintendo would boast two of the series most beloved games as well as one that wouldn't get its due in the West until rerelease much later.

Final Fantasy IV introduced the most significant shift in the series' formula to date, as it increased the number of characters who would enter into and out of your party, boasting eleven playable characters. This built upon what *Final Fantasy III* did with the personification of its characters, producing a cast of characters that stood on their own narrative merits instead of as reflections of the players controlling them. Of course, the introduction of rounded protagonists and antagonists puts pressure on the control that the series promised its players. However, as the characters themselves slotted into specific jobs and personalities, players naturally gravitated to their favorites, and the ability to prioritize certain party members over others or even the opportunity to be fans of specific characters, however minor, opened a new sort of metafictional control to players. It was satisfying to have control over largely flat characters, but as it turns out, being the ersatz Dungeon Master (or DM) of a group of fleshed-out, conflicted characters in a full narrative was exponentially more satisfying.

In this entry, the player is given control of Cecil, a soldier and dark knight of the empire of Baron. We are immediately thrust into Cecil's moral quandary over his role with the empire, as he has to follow orders to steal the water crystal from a nearby village as part of a mission to hoard crystals for Baron. Upon returning to Baron, his apprehension gets him court-martialed, with the only hope of clemency depending on a quest to take a package to a nearby village. The package, it turns out, is a bunch of firebomb monsters who reduce the village to ashes. You're likely picking up the narrative arc of the game. Throughout, Cecil is forced to account for his actions that caused undue harm, unknowingly or otherwise, and he also is forced to work with and make amends to his many victims, in turn becoming a hero instead of a villain.

The game also touches on some of the other themes in *Final Fantasy II* and *Final Fantasy III*, specifically the impact of a friend turning against another and breaking trust. At the conclusion of the game, Kain, Cecil's friend (then enemy, then friend again) must grapple with his actions in exile instead of being killed in revenge or redeemed by noble sacrifice. Kain's moral ambiguity is driven by his characterization: his interactions with other fleshed-out characters make reconciliation or even understanding quite complex. This moral complexity runs through the series' later installments, particularly *Final Fantasy VI*, which increases the number of party members dramatically and as a result has produced one of the most enduring fan-favorite games in the series. But before spending time on *Final Fantasy VI*, I want to touch on *Final Fantasy V*, which is both a compelling game in its own right and a good example of the influence of audience reception.

Final Fantasy V's plot is less ambitious than the plot of *Final Fantasy IV*, falling back on the group of thinly characterized adventurers seen in earlier games as they follow in the footsteps of an older group of heroes trying to defeat a terrible foe. More importantly to the history of *Final Fantasy*, though, is the elaboration of the job system in *Final Fantasy III*, which wildly influenced later games but was not available to Western audiences until a remastered version of *Final Fantasy V* was released on the Sony Playstation in 1999, seven years after its initial release. Upon release, the game received mixed reviews, with Andrew Vestal of *GameSpot* saying that the plot was "certainly not" the reason the game had appeal; instead, the star of the show was the game's "rock-solid gameplay."[8]

The job system specifically was what endeared so many gamers to *Final Fantasy V*, and its reintroduction to the West in 1999 was a useful vision of games to come. Though the specific quality of job development—any character can learn and master any and all jobs, so your healer, for instance, could also be a thief or a ninja—was and is still unique to *Final Fantasy V*, the ability to perfect a party's makeup became a beloved element of *Final Fantasy* games. Whether through job systems, magic management, or the use of specific stat boosts, most if not all of the games after *Final Fantasy V*—and certainly after the 1999 release of the PSX version of the game—include a system by which players can assert even more individual control over their characters. Often called min-maxing, this practice allows for the possibility of many optimized lineups, intensifying the appeal of playing and replaying each game, something that surely pleased Square-Enix management.

But more than a corporate coup—one of many, it would turn out—the job system was something that opened up *Final Fantasy* to a larger socially communicative space. Although older games may have had help forums or tip lines available to answer plot-based questions or solve roadblocks for players, the introduction of min-maxing meant that gamers could communicate and *debate* the optimal way to play their game. This sharing of knowledge and experience introduced another kind of pleasure into *Final Fantasy* that would come to define the series through its sheer popularity with its audience.

* * *

Final Fantasy VI was the final installment in the series to be released on either Nintendo or Super Nintendo, which represents a sea change for the series. These early games are seen as retro titles, appealing in their simplistic design, pixel art, and traditional top-down perspective. After this game, the second-generation *Final Fantasy* games would continue to build new and often exciting visual spaces, but the rapid evolution of plot devices would slow down. Indeed, between *Final Fantasy VI* and *VII*, the shape of the series narrative solidified, and both titles are understandably well loved and much discussed as a result.

Final Fantasy VI begins in a similar way to *Final Fantasy IV*, with the player taking control of enemy forces invading an outpost town to steal their magical totem—not a crystal in this game, but an "esper." What becomes clear very quickly, though, is that your character, similar in many ways to the green-haired magic user Rydia in *Final Fantasy IV*, is not pillaging this town of her own free will. Terra, who we discover is the only magic user left in the world, is being mind-controlled by soldiers of the Empire, and her escape and rejection of the Empire's desires begins the game's emphasis on the rebellion against authority that animates the rest of the game. The Empire, headed by the evil Kefka and Emperor Gestahl, is a technological giant, representing the first use of magical technology (or "magitek") in the *Final Fantasy* series. The specific instances of their incursions into sovereign spaces to steal magical elements that could threaten or aid the Empire are too numerous to mention; suffice it to say, the main goal of *Final Fantasy VI*, outside of character development, is to attack and defeat the unambiguously evil and expansive Empire.

The inclusion of an Empire is certainly not new ground for *Final Fantasy*, but the admixture of technology and fantasy is, and the decision to emphasize this technology as a replacement for an older, forbidden kind of magic would become a hallmark of the *Final Fantasy* series. This mixture of fantasy and sci-fi is less a marriage of genres than a rejection of the firm if fantastical historicizing of previous *Final Fantasy* titles. The kingdoms and castles are still there, of course, but now they fly and share space with mechanical walking robots and futuristic guns. In addition to adding to the set pieces, *Final Fantasy VI* also included more characters than ever before, with fourteen characters that could join your party, spanning from swordsmen to magicians to ninjas and everything in between.

And finally, without going into the massive plot of *Final Fantasy VI* too much, the game leans into more whimsical qualities that the series returns to again and again throughout the next twenty-six years. Characters are introduced seemingly at a whim, and all come with their own tragedies and also their own quirky personalities and combat styles. Enemies range from Kefka, a mad court jester bent on the literal destruction of the world, to a haunted painting, to a train engineered and piloted by ghosts. Famously in *Final Fantasy VI*, you, as the monk Sabin, can suplex that train. And although the game revels in this quirkiness, it also lays on the dramatic quality of previous games, interspersing carnival-esque silliness with the Empire's wanton destruction of entire towns and cities. This rapid shifting of tone allows the player a sort of emotional handrail to relate with the game: when things are good, the player can enjoy the characters and their development, picking favorites and building the totality of the game in his or her mind; when they are serious, that totality enforces investment in the plot, since that plot directly impacts or even threatens her favorite characters.

This ambivalence between humor and tragedy, futurity and antiquity, and control of and acquiescence to narratives is solidified as the *Final Fantasy* format in *Final Fantasy VII*, the game that, not coincidentally, introduced many to the series. Released on Sony Playstation, *Final Fantasy VII* occupies a unique place in series history as the first game to migrate away from Nintendo systems. Indeed, *Final Fantasy* would not return to Nintendo for many years—and never again exclusively—and the shift to Sony's newly popular Playstation offered a popularity that *Final Fantasy VII* used to its fullest. The game is a success now as it was then and has sold more than 10 million copies since its release in 1997.[9]

Popularity or sales numbers aren't important here in and of themselves; however, the popularity of *Final Fantasy VII* matters most because it followed the success of its predecessor and solidified the thematic template for *Final Fantasy* games. The game begins with your protagonist—Cloud Strife—joining a group of freedom fighters (or ecoterrorists, depending on your perspective) who are attempting to combat a technologically fascistic group called Shinra in the wildly Jodorowsky-Moebius inspired future city of Midgar. During this mission, Cloud teams up with friends old and new, and after leaving the city finds himself in a world of magic, combat, and far more rural settings as well as new and unnerving technological ones. Along the way, he loses an ally, love interest, and perhaps most importantly, a playable character to the main villain Sephiroth, who kills her outright.

This scene has resonated with players over time, though less for its pure gravitas (it is, after all, a fairly low-res scene with unevenly characterized action) and more for its contrast with the plot's fairly persistent levity in the face of gritty darkness. A giant moogle robot piloted by a cat is one of your party members; an optional member of the party is essentially a souped-up movie vampire. One of the most beloved areas of the game is a floating casino where the player can race *Final Fantasy*'s most famous bird, the chocobo. These, of course, are the scenes that allow the player to grow connected to the characters via their reactions to the strange world around them and the low stakes of the down moments of the narrative. And these connections provide the pathos when the stakes become higher and deadlier.

In short, what *Final Fantasy VI* and *VII* cement for the franchise is a tripartite model for gameplay. First, the player needs to have a strong measure of control over a series of interchangeable and already characterized playable characters. The choice and control does not extend to the whole plot—à la *Final Fantasy I, II,* and *III* or a *DnD* playthrough—but involves which of the characters get to star and participate the most in the narrative as it progresses along its winding trail. Second, the game needs to present a series of complex in-game battle and progression systems that are mastered either by trial and error or, once the internet evolves into its current state, community guidance. This produces another dichotomy, wherein the solitude of the game's immersive state intensifies when shared with others who can only "assist" from a distance without impacting the game itself. Finally, the game needs to be narratively ambiguous in its setting and tone: it can't be entirely futuristic or entirely historical; it can't be "happy" or "sad"; it must vacillate between these states. This doesn't mean that the games are indecisive—though they may often be confusing or convoluted in their plotting—but rather that the games, by producing a multitude of settings and feelings, again center the player experience. The player can prioritize the aesthetics and feelings they enjoy most, relishing those parts of the game and rushing through the bits they dislike.

And so we're left with a version of *Final Fantasy* that looks like a player-focused, immersive, and ultimately formulaic game. But formulaic does not mean lazy or unenjoyable, and, although the games certainly inhabit a particular genre of their own making, they were able to push at the borders of this genre as fans demanded more.

* * *

Our journey through *Final Fantasy VIII* to *Final Fantasy XIII* is a lot shorter than many readers will like. The reason for this is two-fold: one, I don't want to spend time recounting plots that you could just as easily look up online. I'm sure my recaps are enjoyable enough, but there's not much to be gained there. Second, there's a case to be made that the formula works better when stripped of its context. So, yes, these games are very good for the most part, and each of them offers something different and unique; each also has its own moment in history, which is given short shrift as well. But most importantly, each of these games leading to *Final Fantasy XIV* repeats what we have seen in *Final Fantasy VI* and *VII*, tweaking the *Final Fantasy* formula only as a reaction to audience expectations and not in the progressive, experimental way we've seen heretofore. With that said, here comes the (pun not intended) lightning round of *Final Fantasy* titles.

Final Fantasy VIII was and is well regarded as a sequel to *Final Fantasy VII*. It takes place in a world centered around a military school whose graduates become members of the elite SeeD squad. This paramilitary unit—housed in a floating island garden—is the heroic core of the game and where your party members are drawn from; it is also where one of the game's central enemies comes from, as your classmate Seifer turns from friend to foe, echoing the previous three or four *Final Fantasy* games. The other main villain is a sorceress named Edea. Defeating her requires massive sacrifice and confusing time travel; in contrast to this, the game boasts a frivolously fun card game and a compelling romance plot, the latter of which is unique in *Final Fantasy* games. Still, both operate as palette cleansers from the weight of the main plot, continuing that well-worn tradition.

Final Fantasy IX was developed alongside *Final Fantasy VIII* in a move that seems as much a hedging of bets as anything, as it deviates from the visual and storytelling style of *Final Fantasy VIII* dramatically. The game's appearance has more in common with *Final Fantasy V* than any other previous game, and although *Final Fantasy VIII* leans heavily into the dramatic end of *Final Fantasy*'s narrative dialectic, *Final Fantasy IX* is decidedly more whimsical. It follows the story of a thief and a kidnapped princess, though the plot becomes more metaphysical as time goes on. Indeed, though the game situates itself as fantastical and set in an ancient world, it also devolves into a storyline about the transitory quality of the soul. The final optional boss is Ozma, a huge technologically imposing sphere of pure reflective metal.

Final Fantasy X was the first *Final Fantasy* game on Playstation 2, and much like *Final Fantasy IV* and *VII* on their respective systems, it is a self-consciously serious game. This was perhaps a response to critical reception of *Final Fantasy IX* as a throwback or a reiteration of previous games. As Andrew Vestal of *GameSpot* wrote, "Nearly every element of *Final Fantasy IX* seems designed to trigger a nostalgic response in series fans." *Final Fantasy X* seemed set to shift away from that dramatically. The game focuses on a new series chestnut, the rejection of gods and higher powers, which derives from the distrust of state and imperial power in other entries. The battle system was changed from the complex materia system of *Final Fantasy VII* as well as from the magic system of *Final Fantasy VI* and *IX* to a skill tree that allowed players even more freedom to min-max their party members. The plot was serious, dark, and invoked an apocalyptic tone. But amid its most self-serious title, Square-Enix still provided an underwater soccer mini-game, as well as the *Charlie's Angels*–esque spinoff of *Final Fantasy X-2*.

Final Fantasy XI, the first attempt to make the series into an MMO, met with mixed results. As an online game, *Final Fantasy XI* can be tricky to place in our analysis, but suffice it to say, it expanded the communal quality of *Final Fantasy* fandom from a sort of message board simulacrum to a fully inter-reliant community of gamers playing together. Unfortunately for this experiment, the execution was less streamlined than many expected, and the absolutely crushing grind of the game detracted from the sense of narrative control that had been baked into every *Final Fantasy* game to that point. Albeit financially successful and influential as an idea, *Final Fantasy XI* bucked the archetype dramatically. As Charles Onyett writes for IGN, "FFXI isn't what you're used to if you've never played an MMORPG. It's a game that requires hours of dedication on a near-daily basis."[10] Thus we have a capacious narrative that controls the player and demands too much from them to fit the *Final Fantasy* model as such.

In *Final Fantasy XII*, the paradigm shifts back into a familiar, comfortable spot, a political saga that spreads over several areas on a large map, is driven by multiple compelling characters, and features that classic series mix of technology and the old world, drama and levity. It also had a vast evil Empire as a foil to our heroes and a complex battle system that allowed for plenty of min-maxing. Perhaps not coincidentally, it received the sixth perfect score ever in the storied Japanese games magazine *Famitsu*, as well as near-universal praise from its player base.

Final Fantasy XIII followed as the first on Playstation 3 and represented another attempt at a sea change that corresponded with a new piece of hardware. The game was set in a futuristic, technically advanced world that shifted away from the more open RPG vistas of previous games toward a linear narrative. It also attempted to introduce a new lasting protagonist in the mold of Cloud Strife, a woman named Lightning. Motomu Toriyama, the producer of *Final Fantasy XIII*, described the approach: "players are presented with multiple different situations on the field, [and] in a lot of senses FFXIII is more like an FPS than an RPG."[11] This, unsurprisingly, received negative feedback from fans looking for a typical *Final Fantasy* game as opposed to a reimagining of the series model, but the game also provided players with a robust combat system, a compelling and varied group of characters, and a series of ingame sequels that provided depth. In the end, and after several sequels in the world of *Final Fantasy XIII*, it recaptured its audience. It also revealed something about the series: a *Final Fantasy* game could no longer simply be successful on its own terms, but it had to be successful *in concert with* the previous games in the series. In other words, although *Final Fantasy* games were played individually, they were received as a piece of a massive twentyplus-year tradition.

As such, *Final Fantasy* had become a victim of its own success. Willing to experiment with format early and finding success with its continual changes, the series seemed to be primed, by *Final Fantasy VII*, to innovate for years to come. But as it found its stride, player expectations ossified: players came to expect the four dynamic balances—between history and futurism, levity and seriousness, narrative and character limitation and limitlessness, and individual control and community input—to define their experience. When fans did not find that cocktail, the game's popularity suffered.

So what can a game series do when it becomes too iconic to change and too big to fail? As we see in the case of *Final Fantasy XIV*, it can fail and fail and fail again until it succeeds in doing something new.

* * *

The story of how *Final Fantasy XIV* changed the *Final Fantasy* series is as long and winding as my description of the series' first twenty-three years. Although the impact of *Final Fantasy XIV* can be explained simply—that the game simplified the dynamic of balance in its model by making the player the main character in a richly detailed, almost entirely optional narrative—the journey there isn't as easily explained. So in the tradition of telling a story in order to tell another story, let's start in the middle, with *Final Fantasy XIV*'s own attempt at risky innovation.

Somewhere between the conclusion of *Final Fantasy XIV*'s second expansion pack, *Stormblood*, and the beginning of its third expansion pack, *Shadowbringers*, Square-Enix introduced a new element to the world of its by now wildly successful MMO. In a side quest that was meant to fill time between the two patches, we are introduced to the forbidden lands of Eureka, an island that has appeared seemingly out of nowhere and resembles the Isle of Val, a place that we were assured was tragically destroyed two expansions earlier. Without going too far into the weeds of plot, Eureka is presented as a kind of wild, unexplored territory that operates outside of the typical rules of the game in many ways and promises to answer some of the game's more pervasive mysteries. In theory, it should be the perfect time sink for players awaiting their next bit of content.

Eureka, however, is a polarizing place. Kotaku's Mike Fahey puts it most clearly when he writes that Eureka is "a magical island where players can group together and kill large numbers of creatures for very little reward until they fall asleep at the keyboard."[12] My friend and writing colleague Rob Grant put it more succinctly when he heard I was spending time in Eureka instead of getting to the most recent expansion, the admittedly marvelous *Shadowbringers*: "Trevor," he wrote, "I am going to start researching remote shock collars to keep you from doing this to yourself."

Fahey and Grant are not entirely wrong, of course—the Eureka side quest is the kind of grind that would make the earlier games we've covered here proud, a slow progression of dangerous and inconveniently grouped monsters that give just enough experience to keep you interested but not enough to keep the progression snappy. And if they kill you and you can't get resurrected by a friendly player on your server, then you'll lose a big chunk of that experience you've spent so long gathering. In short, Eureka is designed to take a really long time, involves significant risk and retread, and it only has one mechanic: kill monsters.

What keeps people like me coming back to Eureka, however, is the community that this mechanic creates. There's no way to progress in Eureka without teamwork, and each "instance"—think of it like a specific chatroom, adjacent to but distinct from other similar chatrooms running simultaneously—of Eureka that is produced in the game is full of people who most likely do not know each other and have no real interest in each other outside of conquering the hostile world they find themselves in. And this caveat is important, because although I'm uninterested in adding to the mountain of discourse on social interaction in MMOs, I am fascinated by how quickly people are willing to help others to progress in Eureka, even at great inconvenience. It is all in the interest of slow level building, tedious item collection, and random drops by enormous monsters that spawn every few hours, not to mention Eureka's end-game content: the Baldesion Arsenal, a dungeon whose navigation must be carefully coordinated among around fifty-six players, typically on off-server Discords. The players must time their entrance into Eureka as well as their positions on the map in order to enter the arsenal together, thereby earning a chance of finishing the dungeon. But all of that strange, minute planning through all five areas of Eureka occurs in a miraculously ideal setting with a group of people who want that exact same thing and collaborate with other players in order to get there.

Eureka, to put it differently, intensifies the typical game state of *Final Fantasy XIV*. In this game, like many other MMOs, the player must team up with random people in order to finish dungeons and boss content, and cooperation and party mechanics are encouraged throughout. But cooperation of this magnitude—outside of teaming up with two to seven friends to tackle content together—is uncommon. Add to that the bare-bones nature of Eureka and the stark repetition of the mechanics, and you get a world that is at once more inviting and more repellant than any other in this massive game. Eureka is, at its best, a chance to feel like you're part of a manic rush through a weird world with friends acting as guides and, at its worst, a truly lonely place with very little to do. In that way, it's a microcosm of video games and MMOs specifically. And although there's much more to say about the social dynamics therein, I think what's more important is that Eureka, despite being this weird stand-alone escalation of the highs and lows experienced in *Final Fantasy XIV*, feels absolutely indivisible from, and indeed part of, its continuous world.

Far from feeling like an add-on stapled to the game for the purpose of stretching content and maintaining monthly subscriptions, Eureka feels like a completely fleshed-out component of the game world. It is not to the taste of everyone, but much like many elements of *Final Fantasy XIV* that are outside the main plotline—what players call the main story questline or MSQ—it occupies a space wherein players can flesh out their experience of the world around them in the precise ways they would like to. Or, importantly, they can choose not to do that. Because what's unique about *Final Fantasy XIV* in the world of *Final Fantasy* the series is its sheer scope, which allows it, paradoxically, to most effectively immerse the players in their own individualized iterations of the world.

In other words, *Final Fantasy XIV* feels like a real, immersive world because there is too much content to reasonably complete. The decisions your character makes are not the binary "good" or "evil" choices we see in other games nor are they even definitive choices: given the world enough and time, you could do everything the game world has to offer. In this way, the game world of *Final Fantasy XIV* is much like the real world; the niggling question in the back of your mind as to whether you should go back to school for a new career simply is replaced with the thought that maybe it's time to learn how to do alchemy. The world gives you too much to complete, in essence, because that produces the double effect of giving players something to think about when they aren't playing the game as well as a reason to keep coming back to this one game for as long as it remains profitable to produce it. Square-Enix has, in essence, created a perfectly comfortable Skinner box that continues to be enjoyable in just the right ways. Ultimately, the side content of *Final Fantasy XIV* takes the most important dynamic of the *Final Fantasy* model—the balance between player control and narrative guidance—and solves it by giving the player free rein to choose which parts of the narrative to open and which to keep closed.

But unlike Eureka, the MSQ of *Final Fantasy XIV* is not simply going through the motions of addictive and repetitive gameplay— the main quest is specifically meant to tell a narrative with a beginning, middle, and end. But the MSQ also reworks the *Final Fantasy* model, producing challenges to the comfortable routine of previous games in a way that has come into greater focus in its most recent expansion pack, or xpac, *Shadowbringers*.

Before touching on that expansion, we need to contextualize it in the history of previous xpacs, each of which has brought with it dramatic changes. Although many MMOs change a lot with each expansion, *Final Fantasy XIV* is unique in that its first iteration, 1.0, was a massive failure from a critical and player standpoint: people just did not like the game at all. The reasons stemmed from a disinterest in the slow plot pacing, a poorly organized player experience, and game-breaking bugs. Kevin VanOrd's review for *GameSpot* makes the case against 1.0 clear in its subheading: "Square Enix's laborious online role-playing game is a step back for the genre."[13] The game was so bad that a major reviewer thought it single-handedly set back the entire MMO *genre*.

With an unqualified disaster following the underwhelming success of *Final Fantasy XIII*, Square-Enix was quick to make big changes, chief among them being the promotion of Naoki Yoshida to producer and director of the game. The story from there is complicated, but the upshot is that the game was redesigned from scratch, and Square-Enix retained its subscribers through gameplay fixes via patch and promised incentives to those who continued their paid subscriptions through the end of 1.0. In the end, the game needed to be completely overhauled from the ground up, and as of November 11, 2012, 1.0 was shut down entirely, becoming the rare game that can never be played again.

The launch of 2.0, *A Realm Reborn*—what, currently, is the base game of *Final Fantasy XIV*—came with both an apology from Square Enix CEO Yoichi Wada for "damaging the *Final Fantasy* brand"[14] and an explanation of how the events in 1.0 vanished forever from the in-game universe, like when Poochie returned to his home planet on *The Simpsons*. The "warriors of light"—this should sound familiar at this point—stopped the concluding crisis of 1.0 when they saved the world from the terrifying destructive force of the dragon Bahamut. But in doing so, they also vanished from the memories of everyone in Eorzea, the world of *Final Fantasy XIV*. Your character, at the beginning of 2.0, hears from many characters that they can vaguely recall the outcome of that battle— horrible destruction but ultimate victory—but when they try to picture the warriors of light or even remember their names, their minds grow hazy and they can't complete their thoughts. In essence, the entire 1.0 game experience has been confined to the realm of a world-building myth and 2.0 uses its premise as a jumping-off point before leaving it behind entirely.

And although 2.0 still shows the rough edges, the continued improvement and detailing of *Final Fantasy XIV* is nothing less than unprecedented in modern gaming: an overhaul of a AAA game left for dead rarely happens due to the potent mix of prohibitive cost and audience impatience. And thanks to the introduction of more ambitiously framed themes of faith, imperialist conquest, and moral ambiguity in their next three xpacs, Yoshida and the rest of the *Final Fantasy XIV* team built on their momentum, producing a vibrant, living MMO.

Of course, the success of the game in and of itself shouldn't matter too much to us from a critical stance; indeed, the only difference between the failure of 1.0 and the successes of 2.0 through 5.0 is that the former tells a story about the way that the *Final Fantasy* series fails to evolve beyond its model and the latter tells the opposite. That the split between these very different readings hinges on audience reception shouldn't surprise us either, particularly as *Final Fantasy XIV* operates as a kind of microcosm of the larger story I tell about the series in this book: the initial flop was a necessary condition of the later success, disconnection leading to cohesion through collaborative friction between producer and audience.

And more than that, *Final Fantasy XIV*'s placement as an attempt to rework a dull and lifeless first draft encouraged a kind of dynamism about the *Final Fantasy* lore that—intentionally or otherwise—gives its audience a way to conclude the ceaseless anthology-like trek through new worlds every game. The world you occupy as a player in *Final Fantasy XIV* is reflected in thirteen other worlds, a number that doesn't seem coincidental. Though these worlds are often destroyed and "rejoined" with your world by the antagonists of the game, the overlapping of alternate time lines that hew closely but not precisely to the player's own feels like a perfect illustration of the similar, albeit not quite the same, repetition of the *Final Fantasy* series. So it comes as no surprise when, during in-game massive events called raids, older games in the *Final Fantasy* series are codified in the world and in the time line of *Final Fantasy XIV* as either alternate worlds or ancient history; in the first of these massive raids, for instance, the player encounters cloned antagonists from *Final Fantasy III*, which sets the stage for the *Shadowbringers* xpac, the latest in the series.

Thus the history of past *Final Fantasy* games finds its purchase both within the lore of *Final Fantasy XIV* and within the thematic and storytelling technologies of the game. And in *Shadowbringers*, *Final Fantasy XIV* uses this connectivity to make clear the dangerous effects of canonizing the series, specifically what adherence to the past, comfortable gaming models takes from us. *Shadowbringers* goes about this task by highlighting a world that has been so rid of darkness that it has become suffused with light and must be saved from imbalance and ultimate death by radiance. This lighted world, Norvrandt, is not far removed from the worlds at the end of *Final Fantasy* games in which the player has eliminated every plausible threat and the world itself is carefree and without conflict; yet Norvrandt is also a critique of previous games in the series and their focus on the elimination of anything not attuned to the model in which warriors of light embark on serious quests (with levity!) to stop an ancient (but futuristic!) evil. If the connected raids allow the player to conjure a connected world theory for *Final Fantasy* that enables all of the plots to interact in admittedly satisfying ways, then *Shadowbringers* asserts that continuity and its satisfaction is not necessarily something we should be fighting to maintain. In short, the light suffusing Norvrandt is the light cast from *Final Fantasy VI* and *VII*, whose influence *Final Fantasy XIV* is trying to dislodge.

So where does Eureka fit into all of this? This strange spur off the main story of *Final Fantasy XIV* that rewards old-school brute force repetition over these challenging narratives doesn't seem at first glance to fit the complicating quality of *Shadowbringers*. Although Eureka certainly returns to some of *Final Fantasy*'s classic strategies for producing grind, it also maintains this grind by using the link of community as a glue to hold together the whole. Because Eureka, much like every other aspect of *Final Fantasy XIV*, is part of a unified whole only because the community that exists within it agrees, tacitly or explicitly, to uphold it as a unified whole. The core of this whole is the player—now protagonist of the world of Eorzea, along with every other player.

Of course, every piece of media requires this kind of agreement from the audience to a point; there is nothing particularly unique about *Final Fantasy XIV* compared to, say, Charles Dickens's *Great Expectations* in this way. We as an audience accept that Yoshida's and Dickens's worlds, respectively, are coherent expressions of a singular and contained world. This is at its core what is meant when people invoke the suspension of disbelief. But *Final Fantasy XIV* makes an additional leap: the suspension of disbelief is less important than the acceptance of performativity in the space of the game. In other words, the world of Eorzea coheres because we are willing to accept the presence of dragons and monsters and magical crystals, but the totality of the world—what I called the immersive quality at the beginning of this chapter—hinges on the participation of thousands and thousands of other people who also suspend their disbelief. You can be the protagonist of the game without the mediation of narrative simply because everyone else accepts their unmediated roles as coterminous with yours.

As such, the community in *Final Fantasy XIV* actively participates in the rewriting and challenging of the *Final Fantasy* model, enacting in a performative way not only the narrative challenges apparent in *Shadowbringers*, but also the world building necessary to create the total immersion that *Final Fantasy XIV* does better than any other entry in the series. Eureka is a useful example here because an area like Eureka feels populated and alive only so long as people agree to keep it populated and alive. And although the stark distinction between "fun and populous" Eureka and "empty and horrible" Eureka is more stark than much of the rest of the game, it is not unique in this regard. To give an example: I was lucky enough to attend an in-game concert put on by a role-playing guild called the Syndicate. Members of the group, fully in character, produced music from *Final Fantasy IX* on in-game instruments, while other players sat and watched, applauding using command-line prompts when necessary. The absolute commitment to the performance made the occasion "real" in a sense that extended beyond the idea of "players acting like their characters." If there are moments happening like this all over Eorzea, the overworld of *Final Fantasy XIV*, then they influence the quality of other performances simply because they occupy the same space and the same rules.

To put it simply, *Final Fantasy XIV* works because every one of its players agrees to jettison the solipsism of gaming alone and trust in the intentions of a larger community. The game takes the first step of any larger social interaction in this way and embraces the risk of rejection to produce the totality of participation.

* * *

Ultimately, what *Final Fantasy XIV* provides—and what, in the past, *Final Fantasy XI* and *Final Fantasy XIV* 1.0 attempted to provide—is a kind of layered signification for the player. There is at once the information in the game that is directly given to the player, primarily through the MSQ, and events that are not difficult to complete during the regular course of playing the game. Beyond this is a loose sociality that occurs in large meeting areas like cities or in dungeons when the game requires you to group with three, seven, twenty-three, or fifty-five other players to complete a mission. A third level of signification requires leaving the virtual space of the game entirely and engaging with other players to strategize, plan, or playact; typically, this third level is for the harder optional content in the game, like Eureka, or for role playing and niche use of the game itself.

This is significant not only because it shows the breadth of *Final Fantasy XIV*, but also because it incorporates the game into everyday life. The disconnect between reality and game that one experienced in earlier games is lessened. Now, of course, I could read a strategy guide for *Final Fantasy III*, and I would be communing with people who loved the game, too. And if I searched of minmaxing strategies for *Final Fantasy XII*, I'd be doing research much the same way as I would by going to Reddit to read a guide for farming crystals in Eureka. The difference, however, is that once I enter Eureka, I'm connected with all of the people that I've been strategizing with and forced to enter into a social experience that is going to determine how I relate to the game itself. This is not any different from any other MMO, but paired with the sedimented history of *Final Fantasy* games, the player is granted a series totality. Put simply, although there is *Final Fantasy* content both prior to and after *Final Fantasy XIV*, *Final Fantasy XIV* contains the series in a single massive space, providing a connective social and narrative tissue in a single platform. The player relates to the game by being a constitutive part of it; the game relates to the player by presenting an evolving narrative space with which to grapple.

We shouldn't get too far ahead of ourselves, though; we're going to see another MMO outstrip or outrun *Final Fantasy XIV*. As I mentioned at the outset, it's not as if many of the things that I've said about the *Final Fantasy* franchise couldn't be said about the *Warcraft* franchise; sociality in gaming is not new and did not begin or end with *Final Fantasy XIV*. What *is* unique about *Final Fantasy XIV* is the way that it approaches its goal as part of the series, drawing a complete reimagination of the *Final Fantasy* project of the past thirty years. If the first *Final Fantasy* was not the last-ditch effort of a studio expecting to close, then it was an attempt to capitalize on the fantasy genre in gaming. The way it did this, through much of its thirty-plus-year life span, is via stories disconnected in story but connected in theme; again, this is the

Dungeons and Dragons model, wherein adventures share some of the same generic qualities but are imbued with meaning by the players themselves. What a black mage, iconic to the series, means is not at all contained in the first game itself, but is in fact drawn out by fans, writers, and the looping interaction between them. Each character and each game presents a new chance to build upon these shared themes in a new world.

Until, of course, *Final Fantasy XIV* narratively worked to draw connections between these worlds and changed the *Final Fantasy* model through the formal centering of the player as both dungeon master and main character without mediation. Now, we have a game that argues that the stories and the model alike both lead to this new world online and with other players. The opening of this space offers potential to the player, a way to experience the story that heretofore has been untenable at times and unpopular at others.

Perhaps the proof of this shift is less in my analysis of *Final Fantasy XIV*—which I'm sure you'll agree was compelling and wise—but in the current state of *Final Fantasy*, specifically the games released *after Final Fantasy XIV*. *Final Fantasy XV* is the most recent mainstream sequel in the series, released after a fraught development process in 2016. *Final Fantasy XV*'s story has the typical beats of the *Final Fantasy* formula but mostly has made its cultural impact as a road trip game: four friends drive across the country, take pictures, and essentially come of age. The reception was generally positive, even though the game—the first on Playstation 4—subverted expectations by emphasizing the slower vibe of its story, which felt more like a beat poet's travelogue than a fantasy epic. As Peter Brown of *GameSpot* writes in praise of *Final Fantasy XV*, the game is "a fantasy anchored by more mundane, real-world elements" than fantastical storylines. [15] And although the balancing of opposites has been a recurring theme in this chapter, mundanity is rarely the most praised element of any of these games. And yet, unlike the controversial reception of *Final Fantasy XIII*,

Final Fantasy XV's strange Kerouacian verve was seen as a compelling and fun way to rethink the series.

Most recently, Square-Enix released the wildly successful *Final Fantasy VII Remake*, which as I mentioned at the beginning of the chapter, has sold incredibly *despite* being released during the worst pandemic in a century. More interesting than its sales, however, is the fact that *VII Remake* is a vast revision of what, for almost two decades, had been the gold standard of the *Final Fantasy* formula. Everything about the game from its look, to its plot, to its background characters, to its battle system has changed dramatically. Yet, the game has been beloved by its audience, accepted and acclaimed. You would be excused for reading this as a nostalgic reaction. But the game tweaks a formula and source material that fans, not two *Final Fantasies* ago, would have seen as sacrosanct. Now, it is not so sacred as to be an inspiration, but instead raw material for new experience and new art.

Ultimately, this perhaps oversells the transformative aesthetic power of a AAA title. Indeed, Square-Enix could have released a game that I—a PhD in American literature, not game design—made, called it *Final Fantasy XV*, and sold 500,000 copies without breaking a sweat. But it probably could not have done that and expected a good audience response. The fact that Square-Enix can produce games that diverge from and actively tweak the *Final Fantasy* model and still have their audience on board suggests that a sea change has occurred. Given the history of *Final Fantasy XIV*, no one could say that sea change was easily earned.

But because audience impact often can lead companies to abandon their more radically interesting ideas in favor of conservative ideas that please their audiences, we also can see that games and their creators work through their frustrations with their audience to produce something new. *Final Fantasy* as a series is living in this resolution of the dialectic of creator and audience, and by no means does this suggest that every future *Final Fantasy* game will be good or even interesting. But the process of creation and response developed enough to produce a renewed response from the series creators, one showing that the creative circuit between author and audience is not only productive in games but that it is also not at all one sided.

Conclusion

MANY MORE STORIES, MANY MORE AUDIENCES

Games and the Future

At the end of this book, we're left with almost as many questions as we had at the beginning, aren't we? Well, I hope so, anyway, as that's the sign of a good book: complicating things more than clarifying them.

With your new bedrock of series knowledge and aesthetic consideration, you might be wondering, is this the sum total of the world of games? Have we covered everything there is to cover and exhausted the entire store of video game knowledge? The answer of course is no. In fact, there's still so much on the table that a conclusion feels indulgent. What we might do in this conclusion, instead of patting ourselves on the back, is to consider a couple of other avenues of analysis that aspiring scholars and gamers alike might pursue.

Before that, though, I want to thank you for being here with me through this text. This concept of a dialectic relationship between audiences and developers is not something I was totally convinced of until I started doing the hard work of writing this book. There are lots of critiques that can be made about the method here, as well as the choices of object and topic. But I remain proud of the energy given to uncovering how games operate in these discursive spaces, not just as economic objects, but as objects that have the potential to attain artistic merit. This relationship between audience and author is one that is often discussed in many literary critical movements, but this is one of the first instances the relationship between gamers and games has been considered outside of the purely transactional. I hope you've found it as valuable as I have.

Furthermore, I hope I have convinced you that games have a political potential. There is something about the medium that drives a responsiveness that aligns with progressive and reactionary forces both, a need to produce perfect artificial worlds that engages the most imaginative and fearful parts of our minds. If the right is happy to create paranoid delusions and embody them in shooters or questionable strategy games, then the left must be willing to do so, as well. In the end, there may be potential for political organizing within an RPG or a multiplayer shooter, though not quite as much as traditional routes. If this is true, I think it points to a promising avenue in left thought; if not, then we will have to settle for my favorite: aesthetic insight.

And now, without further ado, I lay out a few new avenues to pursue, some genres to consider, and an inexhaustive account of where games might go to develop further series and further responses in the future.

* * *

The example of *Metal Gear* in chapter 4 makes clear the value of disrupting an audience-auteur relationship, therefore most of these suggestions revolve around the idea of easy audience response. Stagnancy can set in, as can a sense of expected praise if the artist is the only game in town and especially if the artist feels that he has invested too much to fail and he needs the only *audience* in town.

That is why, at the top of my list, are visual novels and their somewhat distant cousins, role-playing games (RPGs) made with the publicly available RPGMaker software, essentially a plug-and-play game creator. Both of these genres have been built from the bottom up, which is to say that although some self-made RPGs—the weird and terrifying *Mad Father* comes to mind—will be remastered and rereleased by major companies, they are mostly handmade by enthusiasts who are unsure if anyone, let alone many, people will play their game. The same goes for visual novels, games that bridge and complicate the barrier between books and video games, interactive stories that sometimes pose choices to the reader and often simply tell compelling stories with engaging visuals. The technical skill and money needed to make a visual novel—a story told with static images, text, and a series of choices—are lower hurdles than the skill and money needed to make, say, a triple-A title. The amount of time and care are often comparable, though again, the labor cost is typically a lot less.

What is exciting about the visual novel (VN) is their popularity. Recent VNs like *428 Shibuya Scramble* have audiences clamoring for translations, ports to modern systems, or both. "Amateur"-made games like *Higurashi: When They Cry* have benefited from word of mouth, organic buzz that leads players to get them however they can. *Higurashi*, notably, released a remaster recently, and though it has updated art, many players still prefer the somewhat raw, less polished art of the original. Finally, some VNs like the *steins;gate* series are professionally made with extremely high production value. These may not lead to instant success for their creators in the same way that the "amateur" games that find a market do, but they serve to inspire gamers and, more importantly, to tell stories.

What is notable about both of these genres is that they are not beholden to a single point of view and that they both have a storied tradition that can be drawn upon to produce more compelling work. The low bar for entry can encourage change and audience engagement on the level of creation, not just response. And the connection between these types of games and another kind of emergent game genre, gacha games, tends to be found in the fan art and fan engagement they receive.

To be sure, this is a more popular genre of game that is less difficult to play, offers easier access, and utilizes the same tropes as popular literature, like horror, romance, and so forth. Looking at the success of earnest yet quirky games like *Doki Doki Literature Club* or *Hatoful Boyfriend* shows the way that their popularity encourages access. For every arch columnist writing about the "weird" pigeon dating simulation, there are three or four players who see the value of an interactive experience paired with text. And perhaps those players will initiate the loop of interaction that we see between creator and audience.

* * *

One of the places that engagement between audience and author could be explored most fully is in multiplayer games. I touched on this in the introduction and in chapter 2, where I argued that the rise of multiplayer made games less easily politicized from these violent military shooters in a deeply unexpected and strange (if uneven) way. But there are many more online games available, including the extraordinarily popular *Among Us*.

This game, effectively the schoolyard game of *Mafia*, involves subterfuge, playacting, arguing, and lying, not to mention a sense of irony and humor in order to put up with your friends trying to get your character killed. But within these spaces, players are able to interact and engage with the game's core components, finding ways to play that exceed and complement the stated gameplay and new versions of the game to engage with and exploit for their own fun. The mining simulator *Deep Rock Galactic* is similar in this way; it allows for teamwork on your own terms, multiplayer that has the capacity to make your friend group into a team, again pushing the bounds of the game to find something new within the routinization of work.

Even multiplayer games like *GTFO* or *7 Days to Die* are often played to and for massive audiences who then engage with that play in their own way. Creation doesn't have to be the end result of audience-creator engagement; indeed, the sociality and convivial nature watching as a group is healthy and offers aesthetic potential. Interpretation can grow from these interactions, too, and this kind of high-level analysis is important to pursue (while we're having fun, of course).

* * *

Simulations are games that I considered writing about but couldn't quite find the words. Put it this way: there is a truck-driving simulation called *Euro Truck Simulator* that allows you to drive a virtual big-rig across the virtual highways of Europe. You must obey the speed limit, you have to get your cargo to the site on time, and you must ensure that you can back a truck into a loading dock. In all ways except the ones that count, it is a job, albeit a simulated one. But it is fun to play and it's freeing to pretend to do that job.

Karl Marx, that most jovial of souls, posited in his work on capitalism that the labor force was alienated from the products of their labor. Someone else is getting the money, and more importantly, someone else owns the means of you producing any labor, which means they decide when you work and how. The freeing element of simulated games—and the simulations run from trains to planes to entire European societies in the *Crusader Kings* series—is that you make the choice about how and when your labor is applied. You decide to drive cross-country and enjoy the sights, and you decide when quitting time is called.

What is the potential of such a reworking of work itself? How might we imagine the idea of a job when it is something we choose to do for fun as opposed to something that we are required to do to live? These simulations won't unfetter the alienation of labor from the means of production, but they present a world where that is not inherently the way things are.

* * *

There's too much to say about the "genre" of independent games, primarily because the category is vast. The genres, ideas, aesthetics, goals, imagined audiences, and more vary so widely that all these games have in common, really, is the fact that they are not made by big companies.

In some ways this is enough of a connection. These games produce a condition under which money is not the sole determinant of game content, in which profit is secondary due to a far lower bar for the amounts invested. The game *Night in the Woods* was a massive success, allowing creators Scott Benson and Bethany Hockenberry to start their own collectively governed games studio, but even if it hadn't, the game remains important on its own terms. The same goes for the brilliant *Outer Wilds*, a game that won a BAFTA award for its impressive game design and narrative. It would be remarkable all the same had it gone unnoticed by all but a couple of hundred die-hard fans.

This truth of this also extends to expensive games, as well, but the corporate structure of the AAA studio makes the pressure of producing a hit even more critical. And so, designers in the "indie" sphere can take risks, fail, and produce unremarked-on gems without as much fear of failure. Perhaps the close investment in that individualized success between artist and audience can create a more salutary version of what we saw in the Kojima-audience combination, a way of developing and encouraging interest and content in a symbiotic way.

* * *

The truth is I could keep going. There are many more genres of game to consider, including virtual reality gaming, sports gaming, strategy gaming, among others. But I think the point is made— gaming is not a limited commodity at this point. On the contrary, the plenitude of games available for consideration by any number of audiences is terrifyingly vast. This book omits Nintendo games, some of the most popular intellectual property games on earth, and I could write an entire book about them before acknowledging the other games I've missed.

In such a landscape, the only way to move forward with our inquiry is to examine the way that we engage with these games as an audience. How does our interaction change these games, make them more than what they are, more capacious? How can it change them in less positive ways? And what of the creators? If we cannot nail down a "canon," then we must focus on thinking about a method for discussing our relationship with them and how that relationship can change and grow.

Ultimately, we can definitively say that games matter as a cultural medium; we can even go beyond that and argue that they have potential as an art form. Maybe even more than that, they represent an opportunity to think about art and its relationship with culture in more expansive ways than almost any other medium. As we have seen, games demand sociality of a kind, even when they are single-player affairs like *Metal Gear*, the hand of the director and creative team is more present and demanding of attention than most films. When multiplayer turns a game into a social experiment, the design and aesthetics of the form itself are taken to their limits but are examined less frequently due to poorly funded arts education (though all credit to the teachers and professors fighting the good fight).

Although we can agree that games have merit as cultural objects and artistic, aesthetic forms, the path toward a progressive future or an aesthetically pure future for games is tricky. I've suggested some paths forward here, and we've done aesthetic work that suggests a cultural path that can be taken: centering the player while emphasizing the hand behind design; taking political issues seriously while mirroring them in game design; and trying to imagine games as their own medium with their own demands and complexities. But in some ways, aesthetics can take us only so far if we want a materially better political future, be it more leftist, more progressive, or simply more "humane."

We need to see games actively court these issues without giving in to the impulse of "after-school special" logic, of being content with simply presenting a difficult issue without delving into it or considering possible solutions. In order to do this, we need to see more explicit analysis of these issues. But we also need to see games companies follow their own progressive impulses: they need to pay their workers more, work them less, and break free from the idea that good art is determined by good sales. There is aesthetic potential in the games discussed in this book, but there is political potential in the radical organizing of independent game collectives like the Glory Society, founded after the success of the political tour de force indie game *Night in the Woods*. Indeed, the reason that this conclusion brings to the fore work produced in the margins by people who do not always receive their due as creators, visionaries, and influential artists is that I consider primarily high-profile games in this book. Although that market vanguard sets the tone for the political potential of games, it also opens the door to art that necessarily can build on and even exceed its political horizon.

In the end, the focus must be on a—forgive me—dialectic balance between the art and the world in which it exists. For games in particular this will be difficult to balance: to hold the world with its demands and material conditions in one hand and this massively complex, time-consuming, and labor-intensive process in the other. But games must do this in order to progress. There is a risk that the political stays in games as a kind of marketized mover while the art trickles out. I hope that the more avant-garde games being produced, as well as some of the stalwarts discussed here, continue to push back against the simplification of politics as a selling point and present it as part and parcel of a serious artistic approach that games can and must produce as they grow as a medium.

If there is a progressive future for games, let alone a leftist one, it follows through this messy and productive avenue of interaction. The good news is that the world seems ready for more.

NOTES

INTRODUCTION

1. Plato, *Republic*, 376d.
2. Plato, *Republic*, 376d.
3. Plato, *Republic*, 376d.
4. "Jack Thompson Returns, Argues That Video Games Are Connected to School Shooting," *Comicbook*, February 8, 2018, https://comicbook.com/gaming/2018/02/08/jack-thompson-returns-video-games-marshall-school-shooting/.
5. Adapted from Trevor Strunk, "'Fortnite' Could Only Exist in a World That's Running out of Resources," *The Outline*, October 3, 2018, https://theoutline.com/post/6325/fortnite-logic-of-scarcity?zd=1&zi=z7bdalis.

I. SURVIVAL HORROR

1. Joseph Ardai, "A Fragment of the Diary of Lt. Col. Lemuel Cork, Found among His Papers after His Disappearance," *Computer Gaming World*, June 1993, 107, www.cgwmuseum.org/galleries/issues/cgw_107.pdf.
2. Ardai, "A Fragment of the Diary of Lt. Col. Lemuel Cork," 107.
3. "Resident Evil," *Computer and Video Games*, July 1996, 176, https://archive.org/stream/Computer_and_Video_Games_Issue_

176_1996-07_EMAP_Images_GB#page/n51/mode/2up.

4. "Resident Evil," 176.

5. Wesley Yin-Poole, "Capcom: Survival Horror Market Too Small for Resident Evil," *Eurogamer*, March 23, 2012, www.eurogamer.net/articles/2012-03-23-capcom-survival-horror-market-too-small-for-resident-evil.

2. FIRST-PERSON SHOOTERS

1. Karl Jobst, "A 20 Year Old DOOM Record Was Finally Broken," YouTube, April 5, 2019, www.youtube.com/watch?v=PwngnOCWIZo.

2. *Horizon*, series 33, episode 13, "Psychedelic Science," aired February 27, 1997, on BBC Two.

3. Greg Gittrich, "Do Video Games Teach Killing?" *Los Angeles Daily News*, April 27, 1999, https://extras.denverpost.com/news/shot0427d.htm.

4. "Media Companies Are Sued in Kentucky Shooting," *New York Times*, April 13, 1999, www.nytimes.com/1999/04/13/us/media-companies-are-sued-in-kentucky-shooting.html.

5. Jeff Lundrigan, "Finals," *Next Generation* 3, no. 1 (January 2000): 96.

6. "Doom Game Review," *Common Sense Media*, n.d., www.commonsensemedia.org/game-reviews/doom.

7. "Medal of Honor Game Review," *Common Sense Media*, n.d., www.commonsensemedia.org/game-reviews/medal-of-honor#:~:text=Parents%20need%20to%20know%20that,enlisted%20in%20the%20armed%20forces.

8. "Best of 2003: The 13th Annual Awards," *Computer Games Magazine*, March 2004, 58–62.

9. "Best of the Year 2002: 12th Annual Computer Games Awards," *Computer Games Magazine*, March 2003, 58–61.

10. "Call of Duty: Modern Warfare's White Phosphorus Controversy Explained," *Screen Rant*, January 7, 2020, https://screenrant.com/call-duty-modern-warfare-white-phosphorous-controversy-explained/#:~:text=At%20level%2051%2C%20players%20earn,the%20flesh%20of%20your%20enemies.

11. Curt Feldman, "E3 Update: America's Army Polishes up Its Act," *GameSpot*, May 19, 2005, www.gamespot.com/articles/e3-update-americas-army-polishes-up-its-act/1100-6124594/.

12. Feldman, "E3 Update."

13. Joseph DeLappe, "dead-in-iraq," 2006–2011, www.delappe.net/project/dead-in-iraq.

14. Tycho, "The Sum of All Stuff," *Penny Arcade*, June 5, 2002, www.penny-arcade.com/news/post/2002/06/05/the-sum-of-all-stuff.

15. Feldman, "E3 Update."

16. Simon Parkin, "Call of Duty: Gaming's Role in the Military-Entertainment Complex," *Guardian*, October 22, 2014, www.theguardian.com/technology/2014/oct/22/call-of-duty-gaming-role-military-entertainment-complex.

17. Jim Sterling, "Why I Will Support Modern Warfare 2," *Destructoid*, November 2, 2009, www.destructoid.com/why-i-will-support-modern-warfare-2-153852.phtml.

18. Jeremy Reimer, "That Time Roger Ebert Said Games Will Never Be as Worthy as Movies," *Ars Technica*, November 28, 2020, https://arstechnica.com/gaming/2020/11/5657-2/. Answer Man, Robert Ebert.com, November 27, 2005, https://web.archive.org/web/20060614021814/http://rogerebert.suntimes.com/apps/pbcs.dll/section?category=ANSWERMAN&date=20051127.

19. Sterling, "Why I Will Support Modern Warfare 2."

20. Kieron Gillen, "Wot I Think: About That Level," *Rock, Paper, Shotgun*, November 19, 2009, https://www.rockpapershotgun.com/wot-i-think-about-that-level.

21. Tom Senior, "Modern Warfare 2 Designer Explains the Thinking behind No Russian Mission," *PC Gamer*, n.d., www.pcgamer.com/modern-warfare-2-designer-explains-the-thinking-behind-no-russian-mission/.

22. Senior, "Modern Warfare 2."

23. Parkin, "Call of Duty."

24. John Phipps, "Call of Duty: Modern Warfare and the Cruel Realities of White Phosphorous," *IGN Entertainment*, January 13, 2020, www.ign.com/articles/2019/09/17/modern-warfare-white-phosphorus-killstreak-2019.

25. Judith Butler, *Excitable Speech: A Politics of the Performative* (London: Routledge, 1997), 5.

26. Nicholas Brown, "The Work of Art in the Age of Its Real Subsumption under Capital," nonsite.org, March 13, 2012, https://nonsite.org/the-work-of-art-in-the-age-of-its-real-subsumption-under-capital/.

3. THE *SOULS* SERIES

1. Oliver Cragg, "Why Dark Souls 3 Should Have an Easy Mode and the Problem with 'Playing to Win,'" *International Business Times*, April 12, 2016, www.ibtimes.co.uk/why-dark-souls-3-should-have-easy-mode-problem-playing-win-1553664.

2. Erik Kain, "No, 'Dark Souls 3' Shouldn't Have an Easy Mode (and It Sort of Already Does), *Forbes*, April 7, 2016, www.forbes.com/sites/erikkain/2016/04/07/no-dark-souls-3-shouldnt-have-an-easy-mode-and-it-sort-of-already-does/?sh=3bdcbead4d75.

3. Dia Lacina, "*Pathologic 2* Is Getting Difficulty Sliders, and That's a Good Thing," *Paste*, May 31, 2019, www.pastemagazine.com/games/pathologic-2/pathologic-2-is-getting-difficulty-sliders-and-tha/.

4. "Interview: Demon's Souls," *Edge*, August 13, 2010, https://web.archive.org/web/20130404134819/http://www.edge-online.com/features/interview-demons-souls/.

5. Simon Parkin, "Interview: Bloodborne Creator Hidetaka Miyazaki: 'I Didn't Have a Dream. I Wasn't Ambitious,'" *Guardian*, March 31, 2015, www.theguardian.com/technology/2015/mar/31/bloodborne-dark-souls-creator-hidetaka-miyazaki-interview.

6. Dia Lacina, "*Demon's Souls*' Soundtrack Reminds Us Just How Transient and Treacherous Truth Is," *Paste*, November 6, 2020, www.pastemagazine.com/games/demon-s-souls/demons-souls-soundtrack/.

7. Lacina, "*Demon's Souls*' Soundtrack."

8. Hidetaka Miyazaki and M. Kirie Hayashi, *Dark Souls: Design Works* (Richmond Hill, Ontario: Udon Entertainment, 2014).

9. "Dark Souls II," *Metacritic*, n.d., www.metacritic.com/game/pc/dark-souls-ii.

10. Skarekrow13, "Iron Keep: A Castle in the Clouds?" FextraLife, June 19, 2014, https://fextralife.com/iron-keep-a-castle-in-the-clouds/.

11. Gareth Damian Martin, "Hidetaka Miyazaki's Transcendent Quest for Beauty in Bloodborne," *Kill Screen*, n.d., https://killscreen.com/previously/articles/hidetaka-miyazakis-transcendent-quest-beauty-bloodborne/.

4. METAL GEAR SOLID

1. Simon Parkin, "Hideo Kojima: Video Game Drop-out—Interview Part 1," *Guardian*, May 23, 2012, www.theguardian.com/technology/gamesblog/2012/may/23/hideo-kojima-interview-part-1.

2. John Szczepaniak, "Before They Were Famous," *Retro Gamer*, February 2007, 74.

3. Jeff Gerstmann, "Metal Gear Solid Review," *GameSpot*, September 25, 1998, www.gamespot.com/reviews/metal-gear-solid-review/1900-2546002/.

4. David Radd, "'Controversial' Games: Dealing with Fan Backlash," *Industry Gamers*, November 10, 2009, https://web.archive.org/web/20091118011716/http://www.industrygamers.com/galleries/controversial-games-dealing-with-fan-backlash/6.

5. Geoff Keighley, "The Final Hours of Metal Gear Solid 2: Sons of Liberty," *GameSpot*, November 22, 2001 (reprinted May 16, 2012).

6. Eddie Makuch, "Kojima Addresses Criticism over MGSV's 'Sexy' Quiet Character," *GameSpot*, October 9, 2013, www.gamespot.com/articles/kojima-addresses-criticism-over-mgsvs-sexy-quiet-character/1100-6414204/.

7. Thanks to Andrew Meyer for this observation.

5. FALLOUT AND SHIN MEGAMI TENSEI

1. Fredric Jameson, "Future City," *New Left Review* 21 (May/June 2003), https://newleftreview.org/issues/ii21/articles/fredric-jameson-future-city.

2. "KOXM Episode 75," *Official Xbox Magazine* podcast, August 2007, www.oxmpodcast.com/koxm-episode-75/.

3. Jeremy Dunham, "Shin Megami Tensei: Nocturne," December 13, 2018, IGN Entertainment, www.ign.com/articles/2004/09/23/shin-megami-tensei-nocturne.

4. Eddie Makuch, "Obsidian Denied Bonus over New Vegas Metacritic Score," *GameSpot*, March 15, 2012, www.gamespot.com/articles/obsidian-denied-bonus-over-new-vegas-metacritic-score-studio-head/1100-6366337/).

5. Emma Kent, "Games of the Decade: Fallout New Vegas Knows You Better Than Yourself," November 27, 2019, www.eurogamer.net/articles/2019-11-26-games-of-the-decade-fallout-new-vegas-knows-you-better-than-yourself).

6. FINAL FANTASY

1. Adam Holisky, "World of Warcraft Reaches 12 million Players," *Engadget*, October 7, 2010, www.engadget.com/2010-10-07-world-of-warcraft-reaches-12-million-players.html?guccounter=1&guce_referrer=aHR0cHM6Ly93d3cuZ29vZ2xlLmNvbS88&guce_referrer_sig=AQAAACYWk6HW-rEzn25fShXKyUaXbZG0rrnygrjflyYZLJWAKl_torFB5K060HAJLmpqs1EnPEM76NUrIvjnKcVMKP2skmPTqmHllfRD3byFI43cWXGEoRaJ3Fhb2QQEPJhqC9M9nQ6r8N-KUmX7EKBD53dxADAQAJoO1lBy2O4Pvyyh.

2. Wes Fenlon, "The Researchers Who Once Studied WoW's Corrupted Blood Plague Are Now Fighting the Coronavirus," *PC Gamer*, March 13, 2020, www.pcgamer.com/the-researchers-who-once-studied-wows-corrupted-blood-plague-are-now-fighting-the-coronavirus/).

3. Derek Strickland, "Final Fantasy 7 Remake Is a Huge Success with 3.5 Million Sales," *TweakTown*, April 21, 2020, https://www.tweaktown.com/news/71952/final-fantasy-7-remake-is-huge-success-with-3-5-million-sales/index.htmlwww.tweaktown.com/news/71952/final-fantasy-7-remake-is-huge-success-with-3-5-million-sales/index.html.

4. Stewart Alsop II, "TSR Hobbies Mixes Fact and Fantasy," *Inc.*, February 1982, www.inc.com/magazine/19820201/3601.html.

5. Chris Kohler, "Why's It Called 'Final Fantasy'? Uematsu Explains," *Wired*, July 23, 2009, www.wired.com/2009/07/final-fantasy/.

6. Steven Hansen, "Final Fantasy Was Almost Called Fighting Fantasy," *Destructoid*, May 26, 2015, www.destructoid.com/final-fantasy-was-almost-called-fighting-fantasy-creator-explains-actual-reason-behind-the-name-292792.phtml.

7. Chris Collette, "Spotlight: Final Fantasy II," *Lost Levels*, December 2003, www.lostlevels.org/200312/200312-ffan2.shtml.

8. Andrew Vestal, "Final Fantasy Anthology Review," *GameSpot*, October 14, 1999, www.gamespot.com/reviews/final-fantasy-anthology-review/1900-2547564/).

9. Andrew Webster, "Masterpiece: *Final Fantasy VII*," *ArsTechnica*, May 7, 2020, https://arstechnica.com/gaming/2010/05/masterpiece-final-fantasy-vii/.

10. Charles Onyett, "Final Fantasy XI," IGN Entertainment, May 3, 2006, www.ign.com/articles/2006/05/03/final-fantasy-xi.

11. Jeremy Parish, "Final Fantasy XIII Is Not an RPG," *1Up*, https://web.archive.org/web/20120206214545/http://www.1up.com/previews/final-fantasy-xiii-rpg.

12. Mike Fahey, "Final Fantasy XIV's New Eureka Area Is a Tedious Grind," Kotaku, March 13, 2018, https://kotaku.com/final-fantasy-xivs-new-eureka-area-is-a-tedious-grind-1823735025.

13. Kevin VanOrd, "Final Fantasy XIV Online Review," *GameSpot*, October 6, 2010, www.gamespot.com/reviews/final-fantasy-xiv-online-review/1900-6280901/.

14. Tom Singer, "Square Enix Say Sorry for Final Fantasy XIV, Announce Staff Changes and Free Trial Extension," *PC Gamer*, December 13, 2010, www.pcgamer.com/square-enix-say-sorry-for-final-fantasy-xiv-announce-staff-changes-and-free-trial-extension/.

15. Peter Brown, "Final Fantasy 15 Review," *GameSpot*, November 28, 2016, www.gamespot.com/reviews/final-fantasy-15-review/1900-6416579/.

ACKNOWLEDGMENTS

As is normal with these kinds of things, there are far too many people to thank, so if I missed you, know that I feel worse about it than you do. I want to thank my agent, Erik Hane, for being a stalwart friend, reader, and coach through this whole process. I want to thank Tony Palumbi, as well, for helping me brave writing a book. I want to thank Andrew Meyer for their unfailing ability to rag on me and make me laugh until the moment they knew I needed support, when they'd be my biggest ally and friend. I want to thank Emerson Wright for being my best friend for about twenty years now, even though I scarcely deserve it, and for being an intellectual sounding board par excellence. I want to thank Olivia Broussard for her limitless humor, kindness, cleverness, and warmth and for being an unmatched peer, collaborator, and friend. I want to thank Talya for her help making me socially out there, and Julian Croca-mo for his help recording my ramblings on digital tape so I could get the chance to write this book in the first place. I want to thank everyone who has been on my show, especially Scott Benson, Olivia Broussard, Josh Sawyer, and Alex Navarro, who have come varying lengths of distance to be there live with me at Caveat NYC (thank you Josh Boerman!). Thank you Matt Dering and Connor Southard for putting up with my fears, boredoms, and bad conversations. And thank you Seth Chodosh, Graham Sigurdson, Mike, Erica, Rob, and Jimmy Wrong for never letting me get a big head. Thank you to Jake Bonar for the wonderful notes and brilliant read. Thank you to Sean McTiernan for talking to me when I needed talking to, for being a friend, and for reading a chapter first when I didn't know if it was good. Thank you to Dia Lacina for the same. And thanks to George for the Eorzean memories.

Thanks to all my friends who helped me grow up feeling good about my hobbies—the Romigs, Josh Righter, Kevin and Michelle Grauer, Steve Mattes, Jon Kieran, Dina Yarmus, Chris Curley and Laura Lobosco, Zac and Vicki Tompkins, and more and more and more. Thank you to my academic colleagues who helped me get through the graduate years—Matt Moraghan, Aaron Finley, Jen Phillis, Davis Brecheisen, Mary Hale, Neri Sandoval, Jon Slusar, and more and more and more. And thank you, of course, to the dissertation advisers and teachers who taught me a lot about writing, even if I chose to ignore their advice about how hard it is to get a job in the academy: Anna Kornbluh, Walter Benn Michaels, Nicholas Brown, Jennifer Ashton, Mary Beth Rose, Marty Rubin, Gerry Graff, Nasser Mufti, and more and more and more.

Thanks to the people who helped me grow this strange interest in academics and video games into something bigger. Thank you to Chapo Trap House for letting me sneak into a live show lineup for the first time ever with the Games Debate. Thank you to all the people who took a chance and showed up as guests on my show even though they had very little reason to do so. Thank you for being kind, creative, and brilliant and for letting me ask you questions and share in that just a little bit. Thank you to my personal online sounding board, the Discourse, who are unfailingly willing to put up with my bad times to encourage my good.

My father is the person I first saw do anything like a book in my life, and so my belief that I could get it done comes straight from him. My mother also fed me and gave me a little refuge in which to sleep and write on weekends away from home during the drafting of this book, but that pales in comparison to the encouragement she has given me over the years. Their partners—my stepfather Scott and stepmother Laura—have been unerring points of strength and humor as well, and I thank them for it. My Grandmama, whom I love dearly and who managed to beat a broken hip and COVID-19 to see this published and who would never admit defeat in the face of anything but a nice cup of coffee when she wakes up, deserves all the thanks I can give her and more. My sister Caitlin and her fiancé (husband now?) Domenic D'Andrea, both of whom radiate warmth and support and took in our lovely dog Ray. My stepbrother Jed, his wife Lisa, and his four kids; my brother-in-law Tom, his wife Andrea, and their two boys; and my in-laws too!—you've been a wealth of color and love in my life. Thanks to my extended family and of course the family no longer with us—I think, especially, that my Pop Pop and Pappy would be thrilled to see me published, even if it's maybe not on the topic they expected.

Finally, thank you to my family, my wife Kristin and my children Tilly and Oscar, for everything. I won't go on here because it's impossible to say how much you do for me and mean to me, but I would give up this book and everything that goes with it in a second if you asked me to. That you did not and were patient while I finished it means the world to me. I love you all.

Anyone I didn't mention, know you are in my heart. Anyone who was mentioned isn't responsible for the stuff I wrote if it's bad. If it's good, they can say they inspired it, and I won't stop them.

INDEX